LADY UNDERTAKERS OF OLD TEXAS

KATHY BENJAMIN

THE
History
PRESS

Published by The History Press
Charleston, SC
www.historypress.com

First published 2023

Manufactured in the United States

ISBN 9781467154277

Library of Congress Control Number: 2023937199

Notice: The information in this book is true and complete to the best of our knowledge. It is offered without guarantee on the part of the author or The History Press. The author and The History Press disclaim all liability in connection with the use of this book.

For my niece, Abigail.

CONTENTS

CONTENTS

INTRODUCTION

I n January 1880, twenty-five-year-old Anna Mary Beetham gave birth
to her first child, a daughter named Josephine. Tragically, nine months
later, the baby was dead, as so often happened in those days.

Barely nine months after burying her firstborn, Mrs. Beetham was
in labor with her second. This time, the baby lived. However, it looked
as if the mother would not. Unable to recover and with her weight
plummeting to dangerous levels, John Beetham and his wife left their
home in Weatherford, Texas, heading west, hoping that a desert climate
would help Mrs. Beetham recover.

The couple was not planning to settle in Mineral Wells, but after camping
there a short time, Mrs. Beetham began feeling better, which she credited to
the area's springs. Years later, she recounted her story to a reporter: "Mrs.
Beetham tells of her arrival here in 1881, weighing less than 100 pounds and
with little hope for recovery." Those she was close to who lived in other parts
of the country called her a "perpetual advertisement" for the healing powers
of the city's waters. Even in the early days, desperate invalids from all over
came to Mineral Wells, hoping that the springs would perform a miracle.
Mrs. Beetham said, "I know [people] from all parts of the country, hundreds
of them, that owe their existence today to the great waters of this city."[1]

However, after she regained her strength and the Beethams decided to
stay in the rapidly growing health spa, it became clear that Mrs. Beetham
was no sentimental fool. Many dying people came to Mineral Wells hoping
for a cure—most would not find one. This meant that even in a time of high

An 1897 advertisement for Anna Mary Beetham's undertaking establishment in the *Mineral Wells Graphic*. She ran the business herself until her son Robert grew up, at which point she changed the name to Beetham & Son.

mortality more generally, this tiny town had a particularly steady flow of sick people coming there to die.

So, Mrs. Beetham became an undertaker.

Undertaking in the United States to 1879

Throughout history, in virtually every culture around the world, women have played an outsized roll in the care of the dead. Some have explained this as a natural bookend: as women assist during birth, so should they be there after death.

According to "Exhuming Women's Premarket Duties in the Care of the Dead" by Georganne Rundblad, "[I]n the United States until about [1870], it was predominantly women who took care of the needs of the dead."[2] Evidence left by early American women in their diaries and letter shows that much of what went into preparing a corpse for burial—bathing, dressing, doing the hair—as well as offering comfort to the deceased's family, was much the same as the domestic-sphere work that they were already expected to do. It was only logical that they would oversee the same tasks when it involved a dead body.

Despite this responsibility sounding appropriate for the nineteenth-century ideal of women on paper, in practice it was hard work, both emotionally and physically. Years later, Willie May Cartwright, who grew up in the segregated South at the end of the 1800s, recalled, "We didn't know nothing about no undertakers then; and if anybody died, they sent for Momma. Her and two other women were the shrouding women. Dead folks is so heavy, it would take three women to do it."[3]

Before the U.S. Civil War, when someone died and needed to be buried, a loved one would usually go to the local carpenter for a coffin and then to the livery stable to hire a horse and wagon for the journey to the cemetery. Some of the men who owned these types of businesses took to the work of funerals and expanded their offerings, combining their original concern with early versions of undertaking parlors.

But the Civil War brought something to the nascent American funeral industry that would change women's role in it significantly: embalming. While the process itself had been invented the previous century, it took a war where hundreds of thousands of men died far from home to disrupt the average citizen's idea of what a funeral was. After President Abraham Lincoln's embalmed corpse took its long, slow journey from Washington, D.C., to Illinois, stopping along the way for Northerners to gawp at his unnaturally preserved face, embalming became a funerary must-have almost immediately.

Since the process of embalming was an entirely new addition to the work of caring for the dead, however, it was not something women had learned by watching their mothers do it. It involved technical knowledge, access to chemicals and more complicated interactions with the corpse than simply cleaning and dressing it—the process was more like surgery, really, a field almost wholly closed to women. Embalming itself was described as a "science," separating it still further in the minds of the public from the domestic sphere. As an 1895 article on the modern undertaking business put it, "The science of embalming…restores the natural expression to the features. Thus the advancement of science in this age has achieved a wonderful triumph."[4]

Suddenly, deathcare was a science, and there were colleges where undertakers could—and eventually would be required to—get a degree in said science in order to work as an embalmer. By taking a trade that had been learned by hands-on experience for most of history and turning it into something people needed to attend higher education to be qualified for, it meant women were pushed out. For years, the closest schools of embalming

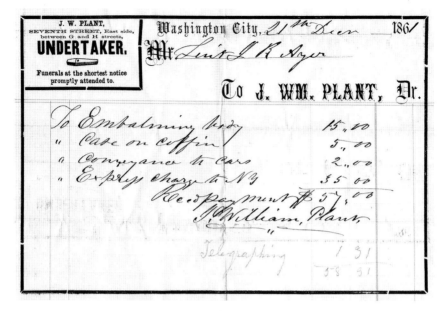

J. William Plant of Washington City was ahead of his time not only as the proprietor of a standalone undertaking business but also for offering embalming as a service as early as December 1861. *UNT Libraries Special Collections.*

to Texas were in Chicago or New York City, which meant a woman would need to pay for her travel expenses and room and board and either risk scandal and danger by going alone or find a companion to come with her. If the prospective student had children, who would watch them while she traveled across the country to attend school? For many would-be lady embalmers, it was impossible.

Three years before Anna Mary Beetham opened her establishment in Mineral Wells, George L. Gause of nearby Fort Worth returned to Texas with an embalming degree and added an undertaking business to his livery stable. While his education was undoubtedly a good selling point with customers, being so far away from the embalming schools of the North and East, Texas was a bit freer with its rules and regulations when it came to the process, at least for a little while. This allowed Mrs. Beetham to advertise herself as an embalmer and perform the procedure when she did not have the relevant degree.

But the laws around embalming would soon change, as would everything else about being an undertaker in the state. Over the next five decades, Anna Mary Beetham would witness significant and rapid changes in every area of the funeral industry.

Part I

THE PROFESSION

Undertaking in Texas, 1880–1899

1886

A few years after Anna Mary Beetham opened her undertaking establishment in Mineral Wells, it became clear that there were enough Texans in the funeral business to organize a statewide association. What was then called the State Undertakers' Association was organized in Fort Worth in late April with thirty charter members. About twenty of them attended the event. The inaugural event included lectures on embalming. In the years before it became a legal requirement to pass the Texas embalming exam, this was one of the informal ways new undertakers would learn the technical process.

1887

One year after forming their professional association, the undertakers met in Dallas for their first-ever convention. This would become an annual event. The number attending doubled from the previous year before the convention even started, with "a large attendance expected."[5]

1893

Two hundred attendees were expected at this year's convention. In preparation for their arrival to the city, an article in the *Galveston Daily News* explained why the undertakers organized their governing body: "The object of the association is to unite all the embalmers and undertakers into a union for the purpose of causing each person pursuing the business to qualify himself in the art....It is expected that all members shall hold diplomas.... The members are required to be temperate in all things and to cultivate a high standard of morality."[6]

Already some of the members were falling at this hurdle. A Mr. Harriman was "expelled from the association for professional misconduct,"[7] while Mr. Stevenson and Mr. Yae were also "dropped from the roll of membership" for unspecified reasons.[8]

One of that year's lectures included a discussion on the difficulties of embalming a 360-pound man.

1895

At the annual convention, the association drafted proposed legislation to regulate the industry, including requiring embalmers to be licensed: "It shall be unlawful to practice or pretend to practice the science of embalming unless said person is a registered embalmer....Any person who shall practice or hold himself or herself as practicing the science of embalming without having complied with the provisions of this act shall be sentenced to pay a fine of not less than $50.00 for each and every offense."[9]

1896

The *Pittsburgh Post* reported that a full decade after Texas undertakers started their association, a national organization was formed. The group's first meeting had a lecture on "Lady Undertakers," which was presented by a Mrs. T.M. Popp.

1897

The *Galveston Tribune* reported that there were about seventy-five undertakers, total, in Texas.

1899

The final convention of the century offered a long and interesting list of lecture topics, including "The Funeral Director's Position in the Community," "The Funeral Directors as Viewed by the Ministry," "Treatment of Contagious Diseases by Which They Become Harmless," "Special and Most Satisfactory Treatment of Apoplexy" and "Mangled Bodies."[10]

GETTING INTO THE BUSINESS

Because women were pushed out of the funeral business after the Civil War, there was effectively a generation of Texas women who no longer learned the care of the dead at their mothers' sides as children. However, the vocation continued to be one with strong familial bonds. Many of this new kind of woman undertaker learned the ropes from their fathers, or even more commonly, they married into it. Wives with funeral director husbands were often involved in the business, even if only on an unofficial basis, although a large number committed to it completely, getting their own embalming degrees.

In some cases, the career included multiple generations of a family. Helena Schaetter (née Koch) married into an established undertaking family in Fredericksburg in 1920. The modern Schaetter Funeral Home records that as the couple's children grew and joined the business, they ended up with the most active embalming licenses in one family in Texas at the time with five.

Alma Ryan (née Jatho) was born into an undertaking family, although her

The lovely and fashionable Alma Jatho shortly before she married J.E. Ryan in 1904. The young woman was a far cry from the image of the old, miserable lady undertakers so often presented in stories and jokes from the time. *Victoria College/University of Houston-Victoria Library.*

ancestry was quite different. Her maternal grandfather "saw service under the great Napoleon and received the insignia of the Legion of Honor of France and a commission as lieutenant in the French Army for gallantry at the Battle of Bautzen."[11] But Alma's father was the first undertaker in Victoria, and when she married, Alma brought her husband, who previously had no experience in the funeral industry, into the family business.

The fact that the business tended to be a family affair meant that the relationships between Texas undertakers was a tangled web indeed. While there are many examples one could give, perhaps the various connections are summed up best with the Smith sisters. In the 1890s, Lilly and Viola Smith married Henry Vodrie and Joseph Shelley, respectively. All four of them became undertakers in San Antonio, and over the next few decades, the couples owned funeral homes both together and separately.

The two women had another sister, Rosa Lee Smith, who married Porter Loring. Mr. Loring decided that he too would go into the funeral business and at one point was partners with his brother-in-law Mr. Shelley. Their concern, the Shelley-Loring Undertaker Company, was listed on the death certificate of Emily Sneddon, yet another San Antonio undertaker, in 1917.

After Joseph Shelley died in 1922, followed by Viola the following year, Lilly Vodrie took over their establishment, while brother-in-law Mr. Loring struck out on his own. One of his employees at the new Porter Loring Funeral Home was Ellen Fischer, and it was there that she met her future husband, fellow funeral director Harold Saunders. After their marriage in 1929, they would go on to open their own establishment, eventually buying the funeral home that Matilde Riebe had founded with her husband, Otto, from its current owner and operator, the Riebes' daughter, Hattie Faircloth.

Not all women came into the business through a familial connection, although it was uncommon. Even more notable than most was the story of Maggie Fulleylove Starks, who opened her own parlor as a twenty-two-year-old widow in 1927. She explained the decision years later, saying, "I didn't care to teach school. That's all a Black woman could do back then. I had a child; I wanted to be with her all the time. It just sprung to my mind to come back to San Angelo and go into the undertaking business."[12] While she makes it seem like an obvious solution, the reality is that what she did was incredibly rare and noteworthy.

SLIGHTLY DUBIOUS FIRSTS

Anna Mary Beetham is believed to be the first woman in Texas to own and manage her own undertaking company and almost certainly was the first to do it under her own name. Even with historical evidence on her side, however, it is wise to hedge one's bets when making any superlative claim about lady undertakers of this period.

A pattern that emerges with the early woman undertaker is the claim or belief that she was "first." Some were said to be the first woman undertaker in Texas or in a particular city, or perhaps the first licensed embalmer. In contemporary sources, this was often used as an advertising tactic for the business they were associated with. In more modern accounts, it is usually a descendant who makes the claim, which is understandable when one thinks of the stories passed down in families that start with a seed of truth and

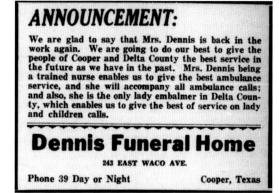

ANNOUNCEMENT:

We are glad to say that Mrs. Dennis is back in the work again. We are going to do our best to give the people of Cooper and Delta County the best service in the future as we have in the past. Mrs. Dennis being a trained nurse enables us to give the best ambulance service, and she will accompany all ambulance calls; and also, she is the only lady embalmer in Delta County, which enables us to give the best of service on lady and children calls.

Dennis Funeral Home

243 EAST WACO AVE.

Phone 39 Day or Night   Cooper, Texas

Having a woman undertaker out of work, especially if she was "the only lady embalmer in Delta County," as the Dennis Funeral Home claimed of Trudy Dennis in 1932, was a problem for the communities that relied on them to prepare the bodies of deceased women and children. *From the Cooper Review.*

become something much more impressive-sounding over the years. When writing an obituary for a mother or grandmother, saying that she was "an undertaker at a time when few women were" doesn't sound quite as impressive as "the first female undertaker in Texas."

While most of these claims are either easily disproven or highly doubtful, there is not normally any intention of inaccuracy behind them. The broader point is that even after decades of women in the funeral business in Texas, there were still so few, covering such a large area, that each new woman undertaker to enter the industry could realistically be mistaken for the first. She probably *was* the first woman undertaker that hundreds or even thousands of her neighbors had ever heard of. Whether or not she was "first" in the technical sense, she was likely the first in her world. To be a woman undertaker in Texas around the turn of the twentieth century was to be one of a very small group.

This is how we get so many competing claims. Women who were given the title of "first" in various records include Olivia Schwartz of Baird ("the first women [*sic*] in Texas to receive a license in embalming"),[13] Elma Beck of Yoakum ("first woman undertaker in the state")[14] and Bettie Lattner of Mineral Wells ("first licensed woman embalmer of the state").[15]

Lattner may, in fact, have the right to that specific title, as after the laws changed to require embalmers to be licensed, she was part of the first class of test-takers—the modern version of her establishment, Baum-Carlock-Bumgardner Funeral Home, says that she was license no. 15, earned in 1903, the first year the exam was given in Texas. Her only competition in this claim is Willie Horner, who also claimed to be the "only licensed woman embalmer in the state"[16] in 1903 and one of the "first embalmers to qualify under the new law."[17] As she and Lattner took the exam at the same time, they effectively tied. Horner, was, however, the "only Catholic lady to take the embalmer's examination."[18]

Other women, or at least those making the claims for them, set their sights on smaller and therefore more realistic geographic areas. This still led to overlap, however, when it came to Lucy Thomas (the "Panhandle's first licensed woman mortician")[19] and Montie McMinn (the "first licensed woman mortician in Childress County,"[20] which is located in the Panhandle).

Trudy Dennis found her geographic dominance growing over the years. In 1931, she was "first and only Lady Embalmer [in Delta County]."[21] In 1933, this expanded to "the only Lady Embalmer in Cooper and this part of the State"[22] and "only lady embalmer in Northeast Texas";[23] the year after that, she was the "only lady embalmer in North Texas."[24]

El Paso, in particular, was a hot property claimed by many lady embalmers as their conquest. As well as the aforementioned Willie Horner (the "only licensed lady embalmer in [El Paso]"[25] in 1906), there was Minnie Nagley (the "only lady undertaker in the city"[26] in 1899 and the "only graduated Lady Embalmer in the southwest"[27] in 1901) and Josefa Estrada ("El Paso's only woman undertaker"[28] in 1930).

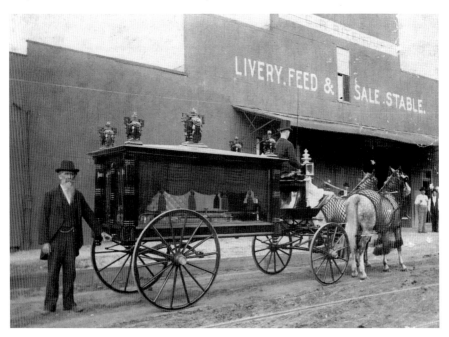

A man, believed to be J.P. Crouch, shows off an ornate hearse around 1890. Emma Parker and her husband joined J.P. Crouch & Company as embalmers in 1915. *Collin County History Museum.*

Bettie Lattner and her husband opened their furniture and undertaking establishment in Mineral Wells around 1892, the first competition for Anna Mary Beetham since she opened her own business there a decade prior. Pictured is the Beethams' first location, before they moved to a much larger premises in 1906. The decorative hearse in front of the building would have been even more ornate when in use, with plumes of ostrich feathers sticking up from the top. *Boyce Ditto Public Library.*

Some advertisements and newspaper reporters smartly hedged their bets when it came to the claim of "first." While Emma Parker was declared to be "McKinney's first lady embalmer and funeral director" in 1915, the rest of the sentence ("in fact there are very few women in Texas who are licensed embalmers")[29] at least acknowledged the existence of others.

In the same way, the modern Schaetter Funeral Home's website concedes that in the early twentieth century, Helena Schaetter was one "of the few licensed women funeral directors in the state," while still declaring that she was "the only one in Fredericksburg."[30] Jessie Thomas was called "one of the first women embalmers in Texas," while Hattie Blessing received the slight variation "one of the first female undertakers in Texas,"[31] although technically these were different definitions, as an undertaker did not necessarily perform embalming.

Jo Ella Livingston's claim to be the "second female licensed mortician in the state of Texas" was a lovely touch, for who would claim to be second if they were not? (She was not, being about two decades too late.)

Perhaps the smartest way to assert their right to a first was to have it be completely unrelated to Texas. Harriet Kreidler, who lived in Chicago before moving to McAllen, was claimed to be the "first licensed woman embalmer in Illinois,"[32] and who in Texas could claim that she wasn't?

PROFESSIONAL ACHIEVEMENTS

Regardless of whether or not they were the "first," early women undertakers in Texas had much more concrete achievements to their names.

Several did exceptionally well in their embalming exams, including Willie Horner, who, it was noted "has received a special commendation by [her embalming professor] for her excellency of work,"[33] and the examining board "made complimentary mention of her examination"[34] in 1903. Two years later, Lena Mahon, who was unmarried and using her maiden name at the time, was also a standout. The *Austin American-Statesman* reported, "Captain V.O. Weed yesterday afternoon received a telegram from Miss Lena Bishop, who is at Mineral Wells attending the meeting of the embalmers, in which she states that she made one of the highest averages in the examinations."[35]

Women in the early days of the professional associations could find themselves one of very few, if not the only, lady undertakers attending annual statewide conventions where those in the funeral business mixed and mingled. In 1899, Minnie Nagley traveled to Ohio to see her family and also to attend classes at two embalming colleges. Not only did she return from her trip with two diplomas from the respective institutions, but she also found time to attend that state's undertaker convention, where it was reported she was the only professional woman present.[36]

In Texas, the *Fort Worth Star-Telegram* reported that Charlie Wright was the only woman undertaker at the national convention in 1927.[37] However, it was not always the case that so few women were represented. In 1910, Viola Shelley was presented with "a beautiful shell ornament as the most popular lady attending the convention,"[38] which implies other, less popular women were there as well.

While Viola Shelley was popular at the Texas undertakers' convention, in his book *Forest McNeir of Texas*, the titular author described her as "the girl I loved best when 200 miles away."

Lady undertakers didn't just go to the annual conventions to have fun and network; some also ran for and won positions on the governing body of the association.

Olivia Schwartz was elected second vice-president in 1905 and first vice-president in 1909. Bettie Lattner, who the local paper reported "captured"[39] the following year's convention for Mineral Wells when she attended in 1904—a big deal, as competition for these lucrative events was always fierce—was elected second vice-president in 1909, meaning that two of the association's four vice-presidents that year were women. The election of lady undertakers to these positions continued when Ella Fall was elected second vice-president at the state convention in 1912.

Katie Lee Childs became the organization's assistant secretary in 1920, all the more notable because she was Black, at a time when the color line firmly divided white and Black undertaking concerns. Fannie Denning was elected the Texas delegate to the national convention in 1925.

The professional achievements of lady undertakers in this area are more impressive when one realizes that a very solid glass ceiling limited their further advancement—a woman would not be elected president of the Texas Funeral Directors Association until Scherry A. Allison in 1992.

TALES FROM THE FUNERAL HOME

Funny Anecdotes

Undertaking is hardly a career that would lend itself to many hilarious incidents, but for those with dark humor, the fun could still be found in strange moments.

When asked by a reporter for the *Hemphill County News* in 1950 what was "the most humorous thing" that had happened in their decades as funeral directors, Minnie Stickley and her husband agreed that it was "the time the gentleman let his glasses fall in a coffin which was opened at a funeral and was afraid to take them out."[40]

Jennie Lou Spalding's father-in-law, who was also an undertaker, told a story about the time a friend of his took a nap in his hearse only to wake up at a most inopportune time. After the friend lay down, Mr. Spalding started a conversation with a potential customer, but "about this time the friend inside of the hearse, having had enough of his berth, kicked open the back

When the Undertakers Meet

MANY TALES ARE TOLD
AND MIRTH HOLDS SWAY

Undertakers Have Keen Sense of Humor and Meet With Amusing Incidents in Pursuit of Their Profession—The Ridiculous and the Tragic Add Spice and Variety to Their Labors.

The revelation that undertakers had a sense of humor was headline-worthy reporting in 1913. *From the* San Antonio Express.

door and poked a foot out."[41] This, of course, scared the bejeezus out of the unsuspecting man, who took off running. This tale follows a common trope of undertaker stories, where someone unexpectedly sees something funeral-related and is terrified. More specifically, these were stories told by white undertakers, with the spooked person usually being identified as Black.

In 2016, Lena Sanders's grandson recounted a story passed down in that family that Lena's husband was once asked to dig a twelve-foot grave for a particular corpse because, he was told, "folks in this county want to make sure that mean [expletive] can't climb out."[42]

Josie Jones and her husband, John Jones, both undertakers in Wharton, had such a great advertising technique circa 1919 that it made *Holland's Magazine* and was repeated in newspapers as far away as Temple. On a local road with a particularly sharp turn, they posted a sign reading, "DANGER! Coffins, Caskets. Motor Hearse. J. Jones, Undertaker."[43]

Interesting Employees

In some cases, the lady undertaker was not necessarily the most interesting employee at the funeral parlor. Anna Beck, for example, employed an eighty-plus-year-old Confederate veteran with a colorful past to tend the cemetery in Yoakum around 1911.

Fayne Hines and her husband, Oscar, also took a big chance on an employee, although one on the other end of the age spectrum. Raby Hampton was just eighteen years old when he and a friend hitchhiked two hundred miles to Wichita Falls in 1925. Despite Hampton having no experience in undertaking, the Hineses hired him. After four years of working for them, Raby went to mortuary school. This history was included in a 1982 article on Raby Hampton, who had yet to retire, and his son Bob, a second-generation undertaker.

Minor Mishaps

There are problems that arise with every business, and with an undertaking parlor, those issues have the opportunity to be worse than for many other types of companies. Fortunately, sometimes they were only minor inconveniences.

For example, in 1925, Ruby Buffington's establishment offered a reward in the *Yoakum Daily Herald* for anyone who found and returned the side walls of a grave tent that had been lost on the way back from a funeral. Fayne Hines's husband also offered a reward in the *Wichita Falls Times* in 1915: twenty-five dollars for anyone who helped catch and convict the unsavory character who thought it was a fun joke to cut the tail off the undertaker's hearse pony.

Annie Ross's mishap could have been much worse, as the *Houston Post* reported in 1899: "A team hitched to one of Ross & Wright's carriages ran away yesterday, hurting no one but badly smashing up the vehicle in running it into a telegraph pole on Louisiana street."[44]

Robberies

While one might expect a thief to rob every other business in a town before even considering breaking into one with dead bodies inside, funeral homes did find themselves being burglarized occasionally. When Daisy Foust's establishment was robbed in 1905, it was still a combination hardware store and funeral parlor, so the thief got away with "two shotguns, two boxes of knives and a case of cigars."[45] The robbery occurred overnight and wasn't noticed until the next morning, when people walking past saw that a metal panel had been removed.

Erected in 1981 by the Texas Historical Commission, Marker no. 8673 honoring J.E. Foust & Son tells a very typical story for early undertakers: a man in a less-specialized commercial endeavor transitions to undertaking with the help of a female relative—in John E. Foust's case, his wife, Daisy—and the business they build becomes a multigenerational family vocation.

Marguerite Underwood, on the other hand, was on the scene in 1925 when her parlor was robbed; she even spoke to the robber himself: "A sneak thief entered the Underwood Funeral Home Monday afternoon and stole about $40 in currency from a desk in the waiting room, while Mrs. Underwood was in a rear room of the building….On her return to the waiting room about five minutes later, she found a man in the room, and she discussed a business matter with him and he told her that anybody, so inclined, could take anything they wanted while no one was about the place. Soon after he left, she discovered her loss."[46]

Fires

In a time of wooden buildings, oil lamps and candles, as well as, at best, a volunteer fire department, it was a fact of life that at any moment one's home, business or even town could be burned to ashes in a conflagration.

Minnie Stickley and her husband lost their undertaking and saddle business to a fire in 1910.[47] They were one of three businesses in the "old Gerlach building" in Canadian, the others being an ice cream parlor and a café. It was the latter that was the cause of the fire, when a gas tank used to heat a coffee urn exploded. The *Wichita Beacon* reported that almost none of the $20,000 to $30,000 in damage was covered by insurance.[48]

It was a suspected electrical fault that partially destroyed the Wall & Stabe undertaking parlor in Houston in 1912, according to the manager E. Joseph Perry, husband of lady undertaker Louise Perry. The $20,000 in damages was mostly insured, but nothing could bring back Headlight, eulogized in the *Houston Post* as "the veteran and highly valued hearse horse belonging to the firm."[49] The couple did not allow the tragedy to affect business, simply using the undamaged rooms to conduct funerals while repairs were made.

Anna Beck was very lucky when her establishment only received about $200 in damage in a major 1917 fire at Yoakum that destroyed an entire city block. Three days later, her husband donated $25 to the fire department in thanks for its efforts. The destruction of the W.R. Brents building in Sherman in 1922 saw Flossie Dannel's business suffer $8,000 in damage.

The year 1920 was a traumatic one for Katie Lee Childs. Her husband, Dan Childs, died on June 8. Oh August 21, she received a check for $500 from the fraternal order the Knights of Pythias, of which her husband had been a member. But less than a week later, on August 26, a fire caused $500

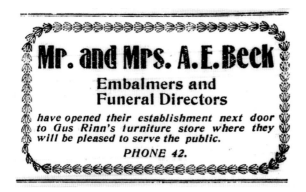

Mr. and Mrs. A.E.Beck

Embalmers and Funeral Directors

have opened their establishment next door to Gus Rinn's furniture store where they will be pleased to serve the public.

PHONE 42.

While most undertaking establishments were named for their location or the male owner, some, like the Becks' funeral home, which opened in 1910, proudly advertised the lady undertaker's name as well. *From the* Yoakum Weekly Times.

in damage to her undertaking parlor, completely destroying the room and its contents.[50]

The blaze that destroyed Susie Hewett's parlor in 1917 was particularly violent, per reporting in Victoria's *Daily Advocate*: "Five firemen were overcome by smoke here last night in an effort to extinguish a blaze in the Taylor Undertaking Company's establishment. They had to be carried from the building, but upon reaching fresh air soon revived."[51] The fire caused $10,000 in damage, but it was not even the first fire to affect the Hewett funeral parlor that year. A previous fire at their home had destroyed three hearses. Despite the double dose of destruction, by April of the following year, the Hewetts were able to announce that they were open again "and ready to serve the public as before the fire," which had "destroyed [the] entire business."[52]

Perhaps the most astonishing fire affected not one but as many as five different lady undertakers and their businesses in El Paso in November 1905. Called "the greatest fire in the history of [the city]" by the *El Paso Times*, the blaze burned for almost twenty-four hours, destroyed a full city block and caused more than $100,000 in damage.[53] The worst destruction was to the large opera house, and the undertaking parlor of Margaret Simmons and her husband was damaged when the walls of that building finally collapsed.

The fire also damaged Minnie Nagley's parlor, although the situation there was rather more dire. As the flames licked at the building, there was a rush to remove two bodies still awaiting burial, while hiding them from the crowd of people who were gawking at the spectacle:

An incident which gave a gruesome feature to the excitement of the fire was the removal of two corpses from Nagley & Kaster's undertaking establishment. When the fire was discovered Nagley & Kaster saw that they had very little time in which to remove anything from their quarters. In their dead room were two corpses, those of Miss Gussie Simmons, a young woman who died Friday and who is to be buried today,[54] and those of Edward Mack, a young man from Joliet, Ill., who died in a local hospital yesterday. The first thought of the undertakers was to remove the corpses to places of safety. The dead bodies, wrapped in their shrouds, were carried out the back way and deposited in a back room of the Popular dry goods store. Later they were removed to the undertaking parlors of Emerson & Berrien.[55]

The latter company at this time employed two lady undertakers, Eliza Berrien and Willie Horner, and possibly also Mrs. W.B. Peterson.

Notable Corpses

Annie Oakley, the famous sharpshooter and member of Buffalo Bill's Wild West Show, was not prepared by a Texas undertaker, as she died in Ohio. But it's often noted that when it became clear she was dying in 1926, Oakley planned her funeral in her last days, including asking for a woman undertaker in Cincinnati, Louise Stocker, to prepare her body before it was cremated. In fact, Stocker was invited to meet Oakley before she died. While the request for a woman undertaker is sometimes cited as an example of Oakley's traditional values, it was not strange for the time.

Lady undertakers in Texas, at least in the period covered by this survey, do not seem to have personally been involved with the preparation of the body of such an illustrious woman as Annie Oakley. Perhaps the most notable case was in 1913, when Anna Mary Beetham prepared the body of Anna Marschalk Randell, the wife of former U.S. congressman Choice B. Randell. She died suddenly while visiting Mineral Wells, just four months after her husband left Congress. While she was connected to an important man, and may well have been a lovely person, Randell is hardly a household name like Annie Oakley.

They might not have handled the bodies themselves (although there is no way of being sure they did not), but some lady undertakers did get their brush with real celebrities, even if the famous individual was dead at the time.

Eliza Berrien's husband had a difficult case in 1894 when Theodore Huston, U.S. consul to Mexico, died suddenly in that country. Berrien's establishment worked with the U.S. and Mexican governments (the latter kindly waived "the usual export duty of $50")[56] to get the body to El Paso, where it was embalmed and prepared for shipment to the deceased's home in Illinois.

The Library of Congress explains that there is not one person who invented the automobile, as so many people designed and experimented with different styles and techniques over centuries, dating all the way to Leonardo da Vinci in the 1400s.[57] However, this did not stop the publication *Horseless Age* from dubbing John Wesley Carhart the "father of the automobile" in 1903.[58] Carhart built a steam engine–powered buggy called "The Spark" in Wisconsin in the early 1870s, before he moved to Texas. He sent an image and a letter about it to the magazine, and it ran a piece on it.[59] Carhart's 1914 obituary in the *Austin American* ran under the headline "First Auto Builder Dies at San Antonio."[60] Mathilde Riebe's undertaking establishment was in charge of the funeral.

Another John Wesley, this one the outlaw and folk icon John Wesley Hardin, was not famous because he was a monster. After a life of crime, murder and periods in jail, he arrived in El Paso in 1894 and proceeded

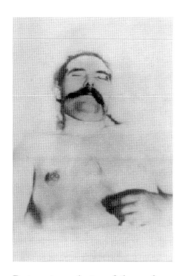

Postmortem photos of the outlaw John Wesley Hardin, taken by Sarah Ross's husband, J.C. Ross, were popular with the El Paso public he had terrorized. Images like this could be bought on the street after Hardin was killed in 1895. *Wikimedia Commons.*

to terrorize the city for ten months. Having arrived in the city with a "kill list" of people who had wronged him, by August 1895, it was said that he only had one person left on it: a young law enforcement officer. The father of the young man confronted Hardin, and later that evening he tracked him down in a saloon. Claiming that he saw Hardin reach for his gun, the older man shot him in the back. The body was taken to Sarah Ross's funeral home, and while it was prepared by her husband, J.C. Ross, she could not avoid seeing the body. The undertaker photographed the corpse for the inquest (it showed signs of many past brushes with death), and by the next day, the images were being sold on the streets of El Paso.

One body brought to the funeral home where Coral Gehrig worked in Dallas is worth mentioning, despite it not happening until 1934. That year, the killing spree of celebrity criminal couple Bonnie and Clyde came to an end in a hail of gunfire. It was Gehrig's employer who handled Clyde Barrow's corpse, as announced in what other newspapers dryly noted was a rather "prosaic" notice in the *Dallas Times Herald*: "Barrow—Clyde C., age 24, passed away at Gibsland, La., early Wednesday morning.… Arrangements to be announced later by Sparkman-Holtz-Brand."[61]

As with everything related to Bonnie and Clyde, even the funeral home had to deal with rumors and excited reporters who wanted to know every detail. One article declared, "Reports that Clyde had paid for his funeral long ago were denied by officials of the Sparkman-Holtz-Brand undertaking company. They admitted however, they had been requested to 'go get the body wherever it might be' when Barrow's time came."[62]

Henrietta Moyer had no connection to her celebrity corpse, except by marriage, but it was still impressive. She wed the undertaker Orville H. Moyer in Pennsylvania in 1903. Two years earlier, her husband was working at a firm in New York State, where, according to his 1947 obituary, "he assisted in the embalming of President William McKinley, assassinated during a trip to Buffalo" in 1901.

The Anonymous Dead

Not all the bodies that ended up in the parlors of lady undertakers were famous. More commonly, they might have no identification at all. In those cases, it was up to the public to identify them. This grisly task was first given to the people of Paris, France, where the morgue became a draw for locals and tourists alike, including the author Charles Dickens. While some identifications did result from the crowds filing past the corpses, most came just for the macabre spectacle.

In 1912, two boys were hunting in the woods when they came across a kind of carcass they were not expecting: the long-dead body of a man, naked and decapitated. The *Mineral Wells Index* reported that the body showed signs of significant animal predation as well. With no indication who the deceased was and no clues to go on, the body was brought to Anna Mary Beetham's funeral parlor in town in the hopes that someone, anyone had an idea who the dead man was. The local populace turned out in droves: "The remains were turned over to Beetham & Son and were Saturday viewed by hundreds of people. The questions are: Who was he? How did he meet his death? And when? The man was evidently killed and the body placed where it was found after the head and clothing had been removed."[63] While some locals reported an incident involving two strange men who might have shot their companion, it's not clear if the body was ever identified.

It's also not clear why two men who died in a jail in Katy in 1924 were not identifiable, but as they had only been arrested a few hours before they died, apparently the police must not have gotten their particulars yet. They died in a fire, and an inquest would later find that one of the two men had set it. Despite the bodies being badly burned, they were brought to Lennora Weadock's funeral home in the hopes that the public could identify them. Leo Weadock received tips from all over the country, and one woman traveled from Chicago believing that one of the men might be her son. But these attempts at identification, as well as the "constant stream" of locals who came to view the bodies, proved fruitless.[64] To avoid burying the men in a pauper's field, a fund was raised to pay for a traditional funeral. At the graves, the minister eulogized, "We know not the homes of these dear departed brothers, but we do know that some time, somewhere, some mothers' hearts have longed and will long for their boys."[65]

In at least one case, an unidentified body at a Texas lady undertaker's parlor was not buried, nor was it cremated. In 1917, a man dying of tuberculosis came to Waxahachie hoping for treatment, but he died a few days later. It became clear that the name he used in town was fake, and like with other unidentified bodies, he was embalmed and displayed in Jennie Lou Spalding's parlor. When the body went unclaimed, instead of laying it to rest in a pauper's field, the funeral home simply kept it on display… for eleven years. Given the moniker "Ikey," he was called by the *Waxahachie Daily Light* one of the town's "most widely known citizens."[66] During that time, attempts continued to be made to learn who the man really was. But in 1928, when a Kansas City museum offered to take Ikey and make him one of its permanent exhibits, the Spalding Undertaking Company agreed and shipped him off.

Major Disasters

A busy day for a Texas lady undertaker might involve dealing with one or even two bodies. But sometimes, when a major disaster hit the state, the number of corpses, and the manner in which they died, could be overwhelming.

Just before 9:00 a.m. on March 18, 1912, San Antonio was rocked by "one of the most terrific boiler explosions in history." While the papers reveled in giving their readers the gory details wrought by the accident, the sad fact was that twenty-six people were killed outright and forty were injured. And the number of casualties was made more difficult to estimate due to the condition of the remains. Mathilde Riebe's funeral home took charge of six dead bodies, as well as "two caskets of parts."[67]

A tornado that hit Frost with no warning in 1930 was "the greatest tragedy in the history of Navarro County" until that point. While contemporary newspaper accounts disagree on the number of victims, reporting numbers from seventeen to twenty-two dead, it's clear that the death toll was shocking. Hattie Beene's parlor took charge of twelve of the bodies. Her husband spoke to the *Corsicana Semi-Weekly Light*, which reported that "[p]reparations were being made Wednesday for a great mass funeral for all the victims of the tornado."[68] Those preparations included getting the debris from the tornado out of the cemetery so that burial was even possible. Despite the claim that this funeral was for "all" the victims, what it really meant was the white victims—the joint funeral did not include eight Black and one Mexican victim who were in the town morgue.[69]

As any Texas funeral director who worked through the COVID-19 pandemic can attest, disease outbreaks can quickly overwhelm the death industry's infrastructure. The 1918 flu pandemic was a major disaster in Texas. In December 1918, the State Board of Health outlined just how serious the situations was: "During the month of October, a hundred and twenty-eight thousand cases were reported in Texas alone, and six thousand deaths were caused by Influenza and pneumonia. Undertakers were unable to supply coffins, and many bodies were buried in pine boxes without any death or burial permit."[70]

The newspapers from the time record glimpses of some of the victims of the flu pandemic who passed into the care of Texas's women undertakers. In Canadian, so many were ill that a field hospital was set up in the headquarters of the Woman's Christian Temperance Union. As they died, the bodies were taken straight from there on stretchers to Minnie Stickley's establishment. Of the twenty deaths listed in the obituary section of the *El Paso Herald* on October 8, 1918, fourteen of them were attributed to influenza and one to pneumonia. The other five gave no cause of death. The Peak Undertaking Company, where Grace Peak assisted her brother, had charge of eleven of the influenza victims and the pneumonia victim—twelve dead from the pandemic in just a few days, and those from just one of El Paso's many funeral homes. Lucile Gunter's Citizens Mortuary in Dallas buried a sixty-eight-year-old woman who died from influenza in February 1919; the *Dallas Express* called her "an easy victim for that dreadful disease."[71]

Controversies

The death of a loved one is always a time of heightened emotions for those left behind to deal with the arrangements. Add to that the high cost of funerals—even around the turn of the twentieth century—the need for everything about laying someone to rest be *perfect* and the involvement of the government, and it can lead to controversy or even legal action. Other times, the undertakers just majorly screw up.

In 1899, a cruel policy caused a scandal in Houston. A Black woman who had just lost her young child went to Ross & Wright, where lady undertaker Annie Ross worked, although there is no evidence that she was part of this disgraceful event. The woman, who was poor, asked Charles Wright to come get the body of her child. He, in turn, told her that she needed to transport her dead child to the undertaking establishment herself.

When the *Houston Post* received a tip about this, a reporter demanded an explanation from the city health officer, Dr. Massie, who said, "Mr. Wright of the undertaking firm of Ross & Wright, county undertakers, has told me...that under his contract with the county the bodies of pauper children must be brought to him. I do not at all approve of the practice. The carrying

Nettie Mhoon, wife of Milus C. Mhoon, pictured with her brother-in-law Willie in either Honey Grove, Texas, or Durant, Oklahoma, circa 1905. The Mhoons moved their business to the latter state after going bankrupt.

of dead babies through the streets in baskets or wrapped in blankets is, in my opinion, barbarous."

Wright did not help himself when a reporter asked him for comment and Wright was a complete and uncaring jerk about the situation. He said that he did not remember the specific incident because "we have cases of that sort every day." Nor was he at all touched by the humanity of the situation, complaining that "this seems to be a great deal of fuss in this case about nothing, particularly when the same custom has been in vogue for the past eighteen months and we have had no trouble about it.…There is no great harm done in bringing [dead children] down here in a covered basket or wrapped in a blanket and very few complain of it."

Of course, it turned out that the entire policy was down to money. Having won the city's contract to bury paupers with a bid of twenty-five cents per burial, Wright then claimed that the price the firm had agreed to wasn't really enough: "We can't be expected to do a great deal for a quarter of a dollar."[72]

The burial of paupers was a continual issue for cities and towns. The San Antonio firm that employed lady undertaker Annie Ludwig won the contract for that city in 1904 with a shockingly low bid: "The pauper dead of San Antonio are to be laid away for the next 12 months by the San Antonio Undertaking and Embalming company for 1 cent apiece, funeral complete."[73] However, that price seems to have led to cutting corners immediately, as "[f]or digging a pauper's grave shallower than the contract called for, Albert Ludwig of the San Antonio Undertaking and Embalming company was fined $10."[74]

Minnie Nagley's establishment buried many of the patients who died at a local hospital, including those who could not afford a funeral. When a member of the public charged at an El Paso City Council meeting that paupers from the hospital were having their clothes stolen before burial, both those at the hospital and the undertaking company were confused. "All I can say," Minnie's husband, J.E. Nagley, told the *El Paso Times*, "is that I have never failed to receive the clothing of every person whom I have buried, such as it was.…The bodies, it is true, are always sent to us undressed, as with cases from all hospitals, but the clothing has always been sent with it."[75]

If undertakers were not caught up in a pauper controversy, they might find themselves being questioned about the treatment of the bodies of convicts. In 1912, a prisoner was shot and killed by a guard in Dallas. The man was buried at a poor farm while his family was contacted. The *Lancaster Herald* reported

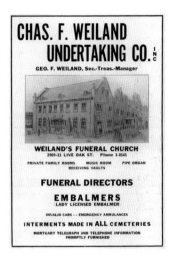

Despite the two men's names at the top of this full-page ad in the 1928 Dallas City Directory, Cora May Weiland, the widow of Charles and sister-in-law of George, was the owner as well as the "lady licensed embalmer." *John F. Worley Directory Company/ Dallas Public Library.*

there were rumors the prisoner had been given an "inhuman burial." Cora Weiland's husband, Charles Weiland, was in charge of exhuming the body and moving it to the cemetery selected by the family. He reassured those concerned that "[u]pon opening the coffin we found that he was dressed in a clean suit of underwear and top shirt and wrapped in a clean bleached white sheet. He was not buried by the authorities in a pauper coffin or in a convict suit as has been stated."[76]

Dora Dobbins's husband was not so lucky when the body of a young girl he had buried was exhumed in 1927. The girl's father wanted the body moved from Borger and claimed that Clyde Dobbins refused. When another undertaker agreed to the task, those present said they were greeted with a horrible sight: "A casket several inches too short for the child's body had been used, it was found, and the legs were said by witnesses to have been broken, presumably as a result of the body's being forced into the casket. The head was hunched forward. According to the coroner who viewed the body today, the body had not been embalmed, though the odor of an embalming fluid could be detected. There was no shroud, a night gown being used in place of one."[77]

Clyde was arrested, and the *Amarillo Globe-Times* reported, "The affair has stirred Borger as few things in the community's brief and hectic history have stirred it."

However, soon the paper had to clarify that "Some Reports in Connection with the Case Are Not Substantiated": "The report that the body had not been embalmed also appears unjustified, but the embalming was found...to have been very imperfectly done."[78]

Dora—who, it can be assumed, was in charge of the embalming, as it involved a child—was not mentioned or charged. The shame was probably punishment enough for her, however, as the papers had a field day and the story was covered far beyond their town.

In the end, the indictment was quashed "on the ground that evidence was insufficient to warrant prosecution."[79] The child's parents sued Clyde after charges were dropped, but by then, according to the *Amarillo Globe-Times*, "Dobbins has closed his funeral parlor in Borger and is said to have moved to some point in Colorado."[80]

Deaths Close to the Funeral Home

Undertakers expect to see death—it's kind of built into the job description. But when death comes unexpectedly to someone connected to the business or even in the funeral home itself, it can be shocking even to those who are used to the experience.

In 1926, Flossie Dannel's husband witnessed one of the strangest deaths ever connected with a Texas undertaker. The *Fort Worth Star-Telegram* tried to sum up the strange story with the headline "Man Kills Self at Morgue After Failure 5 Months Ago to Do So."[81]

Frank Kote was seventy-two and evidently determined to die by suicide in a very specific manner. He went to a Dallas undertaker in July 1925 and spent time picking out a coffin and burial outfit before attempting suicide there and then. He survived and recovered from his injuries.

It was January of the next year when Kote went to another undertaking establishment, this time in Sherman, in the middle of the night. Not worrying about selecting a coffin this time, he rang the bell and again attempted suicide. This time, he succeeded. Responding to the bell, Flossie's husband, John, found the body.

A former employee of Charlie Wright's establishment was murdered by a jilted suitor in 1929. Lola Beatrice Roller King was just eighteen when she was murdered by her forty-five-year-old ex-boyfriend. Her aunt, Ruby Hempkins, and uncle, H.L. Hempkins, both witnessed the shooting, and her uncle then shot and killed the assailant in self-defense. Her aunt told the *Waxahachie Daily Light* that her niece has been "attending school, and working in off hours. She was a stenographer for the Wright Undertaking company, but gave up that place to get away from the doctor. She told me that was afraid of him....Lola did not intend to stay here but a few days and was going to Dallas to get away from the man."[82]

Queen East's Texarkana establishment lost two employees in one violent act in 1930. The two young men—Lester Cooper, twenty-one, and Paul Hunter, twenty-three—had been roommates for years and "had been the best of friends up to the time they engaged in a fist fight" the morning of the tragedy. After the fight, Cooper lay down on his bed for a short while before suddenly getting up, grabbing a gun and shooting Hunter dead. The *Mount Pleasant Daily Times* told its readers that "[t]he report was quite a shock…as Lester had always been a quiet young man, with a pleasant disposition, and he must have been laboring under an unusual strain to have committed such an act."[83]

Some undertaking establishments lost employees to suicide. In 1901, Charles Flocke, the manager of the funeral home owned by Ottilie Baumgarten and her husband, died by suicide at age forty. The *La Grange Journal* reported that the tragedy occurred "owing to embarrassing conditions which seemed insurmountable to him."[84]

Esther Hagedon also had an employee of her parlor die by suicide. In 1930, Jose Pinera was thirty-nine and had evidently been deeply affected by losing most of his family members within only a few years—all to tuberculosis, according to the *El Paso Times*. After his employee's death, Barry Hagedon told the newspaper that Pinera was convinced he also had tuberculosis, despite no signs he actually did.

A profile of J.P. Gunter, the proprietor of the Citizens Mortuary and Undertaking Company, in the paper in July 1919 called him "one of Dallas' leading funeral directors" and listed his accomplishments and positions, including president of his undertaking business and its associated burial society, secretary of the Undertakers Association of Texas, president of his own embalming school and a professor there, a member of the Negro Business League of Texas, a church deacon and a member of many local lodges.[85] So it was quite a shock to the community when, only four months after that profile appeared, his wife, Lucile Gunter, who was also an undertaker at the mortuary, shot him. He died later that day of his wounds, and she was arrested. It is unclear what Lucile's motive was or what happened to her. Lady undertaker Millie Brown and her husband subsequently took over management of Citizens Mortuary.

Alma Johnson's establishment, the Johnson Funeral Home in San Angelo, had been open for only six weeks when one of the company's ambulances hit and killed an eleven-year-old child in July 1929. The ambulance was speeding to a case of a broken leg when it ran over the child, who was in the street. In September, the funeral home was part of a local campaign encouraging motorists to drive safely. However, this was not enough to keep it from being sued by the child's family in October.

It is rather confusing to a modern perspective that for decades, ambulances were the responsibility not of hospitals or other medical establishments but rather came under the purview of undertakers. In fact, some ambulances

A generation of Texans must have found it rather unsettling to see the services of lady embalmer Lorena Brulin touted in the same advertisement an ambulance service. The association was, after all, not a positive one. *U.S. Marine Band Concert Program and Beaumont Fire Department 1929 Yearbook/Fire Museum of Texas.*

were combination hearses. This would be enough to terrify anyone unwell but still alive and kicking inside one; however, it was quite convenient for the funeral home. After all, if a patient died, the vehicle effectively transformed from an ambulance to a hearse instantaneously.

One of the worst ironies of the ambulances run by funeral homes was the fact that pedestrians being injured or killed by the one of the cars was not as uncommon as one would hope. Before speaking at the annual Texas undertakers' convention in 1926, Charles W. Fletcher,[86] a funeral car insurance representative, told the *Fort Worth Star-Telegram*, "The lives of victims are often endangered by unnecessary risks taken by drivers. A check of accidents in which ambulances have figured in Fort Worth and Dallas will substantiate my statements." He believed that the solution was to take the responsibility of ambulance service away from the funeral industry.

CREMATION

In twenty-first-century Texas, cremation has ceased to be controversial. While slightly behind the 2021 national rate of 57.5 percent, in 2022, the state crossed the 50 percent threshold for the first time, with just over half of end-of-life services involving cremation.[87] But before 1930, cremation in Texas was extremely uncommon.

This is not to say that some in Texas were not promoters of the process. The year 1885 saw the founding of the San Antonio Cremation Society, a type of organization that was still so rare its existence merited reports in newspapers across the United States. However, at the same time, "a prominent undertaker" of San Antonio trashed the procedure, saying, "Cremation, in theory, is very good, but the public have not been educated up to it at present...there is an invincible repugnance to subjecting the body of a friend to be burnt up, and the handful of calcined lime that is the residue of cremation does not console the average person to the same extent that the knowledge that the body is preserved intact as long as possible."[88]

Texans seemed to agree with this assessment, as, indeed, did most of the country. At the end of 1897, the *Austin American-Statesman* reported there were twenty-four crematories in the entire United States, which, combined, had incinerated only six thousand bodies total at that point. By 1910, the *Fort Worth Star-Telegram* said these numbers had increased to fifty crematories in the country that handled four thousand cremations every year.

However, the Texas Undertakers Association was, in general, against this new way of doing things, probably because it was much cheaper than burial, if we are to be honest about it. But this was not the line the association used with the public. Instead, men like W.H. Atwell, U.S. attorney for the Northern District of Texas, speaking at the 1912 convention, declared, "In my opinion, cremation is a step toward savagery instead of an advancement toward civilization."

While cremation slowly made inroads in Texas, the still-uncommon practice and the relative rarity of women undertakers meant there are few stories where the two overlap. One exception occurred in 1912, when the *Weekly Advocate* reported that Kate Lowe's establishment had received the cremains

Evergreen Cemetery in Victoria, pictured in 1910. Two years later, the burial ground would see its first interment of cremains, a rarity in Texas at the time. *J.D. Mitchell/Victoria College/ University of Houston-Victoria Library.*

of a woman who had died in California and which were shipped from there to her home of Victoria, Texas. Lowe was to bury them in the grave of the woman's late husband, who had been laid to rest more traditionally at the city's cemetery. It was noted that this was the first time that cremains would be interred in Victoria.[89]

Part II

THE PREJUDICE

Undertaking in Texas, 1900–1919

By the end of the nineteenth century, it was clear that the undertaking business in Texas was just that, a legitimate, moneymaking business that was booming. Both the state organization and the government realized this meant there needed to be changes and regulations to keep control over the industry.

In the midst of these rapid changes, the "otherness" of both women and Black undertakers in Texas (and, as is so often the case, the double bias Black women encountered) came to the forefront in legislation, media and popular

A group photo of attendees to the 27th Texas Funeral Directors Association Convention in 1913. Three women are visible, and records indicate that two of them are most likely Ella Fall and Bettie Lattner. *From the* San Antonio Express.

culture in the first two decades of the twentieth century. While the funeral industry in Texas tried to move forward and modernize, it took a huge step backward with the overt exclusion of Black undertakers from the business of their white counterparts. Forced to go their own way to receive the education necessary to practice and to find business in their communities, Black undertakers formed their own organizations.

1903

This was one of the most important years in this two-decade period, if not in all of Texas funeral history. The Texas Funeral Directors and Embalmers Association saw a huge influx of members because of a change in the law. Effective immediately, embalmers working in Texas had to pass an official exam given by the just-created State Board of Embalming. This was not something they could be grandfathered into—while undertakers who did not embalm bodies were exempt, anyone claiming to be an embalmer, even if they had been embalming corpses on the battlefields of the Civil War, must pass the exam to retain a license.

This was something the undertaker association had been working toward for almost a decade. At the 1894 convention, the body put together draft legislation that would require undertakers to receive education on how to handle diseased corpses, in order that they might keep the wider population safe. The next year, 1895, a more detailed draft bill specifically called for undertakers who offered embalming to register with the state. Interestingly, this draft legislation was gender-inclusive, making clear that it encompassed "any person who shall practice or hold himself or herself as practicing the scient of embalming." While lady embalmers might still be a rarity to the outside world, within the organization, they were acknowledged as a significant and necessary presence.

It is no coincidence that the same year the embalming license laws went into effect in Texas, Black funeral directors formed the Colored Undertakers Association. While barred from most areas of white funeral directing, they were not excluded from the law.

1912

The National Undertakers Association officially banned Black members.

1917

The Colored Undertakers Association of Texas offered its first course of educational lectures.

1919
At a time when local Texas militias routinely threatened to lynch members of the Industrial Workers of the World, Ray Fogle, the husband of woman undertaker Jeanette Fogle, formed the first known union for funeral directors in the United States when he organized the Undertakers and Embalmers' Union No. 16866 in Houston.

THE 1900 AND 1910 U.S. census evidently shocked newspaper reporters, and presumably the population at large, as they realized that women had jobs. Some of those jobs were not even acceptable ones, like teacher or maid, but in areas formerly considered exclusively men's domain. Perhaps enough time had passed for the new generation to forget that many of their grandmothers would have been the local shrouding women, but the fact that lady undertakers existed in the early years of the twentieth century was a fact deserving of inclusion in many a paper.

From the May 31, 1907 *Oklahoma State Labor News*: "Uncle Sam's daughters have shown themselves to be the most advanced, capable and courageous of all womankind. There seems to be nothing under the sun that the American woman can't do if she but makes up her mind to do it....When the last census was taken, 130 different occupations were given and women were represented in [almost] all of them....There are several hundred women undertakers."

From the August 28, 1912 *Edmonton Journal*: "A United States census return makes us realize to what an extent women have invaded the occupations of men. It shows that they are engaged in practically every calling. There are 320 women undertakers in the country."[90]

From the June 23, 1912 *Springfield News-Leader*: "Women as undertakers. How shivery and creepy and unfeminine it seems! Can it be possible that our repugnance is only prejudice? We have to remember that woman doctors and lawyers once seemed a horrible impossibility....Why, after all, is the profession so much different from nursing, which is supposed to be the ideal calling for women? It is all a matter of human service."[91]

As the world at large started to notice and marvel that women undertakers existed, some enterprising Texas journalist decided to learn more about these strange creatures by going straight to the source.

NATIONAL PROFILE: "WOMEN UNDERTAKERS OF TEXAS NUMBER 13 AND ARE VERY SUCCESSFUL"

In the summer of 1912, an article on women undertakers of Texas was syndicated, in one form or another, in newspapers across the country, including the *Fort Worth Record and Register*, the *San Antonio Express*, the *Washington Times*, the *Detroit Free Press*, the *Virginian-Pilot* and the *East Oregonian*.

While the article—and many of the headlines the different papers selected to accompany it—reported that there were thirteen women undertakers in Texas, at no point did any of the editors of those papers actually count the number of names in their own article. In fact, fifteen women were profiled (and of course, there were more women undertakers than either number reflected in the state at that time): Ottilie Baumgarten of Schulenburg; Anna Beck of Yoakum; Gertrude Ellis of Toyah; Willie Horner of El Paso; Bettie Lattner of Mineral Wells; Lena Mahon (née Bishop) of Marfa and, previously, Austin; Olivia Schwartz of Baird; Margaret Simmons of El Paso; Josie P. Smith of Dallas; Mrs. Jack Taylor of Beaumont; Lucy Thomas of Canyon City; Charlie Wright of Temple; Lucinda Wheeler of El Campo; Ella Fall of Waco; and M.A. Clark of Clarksville, the one woman of color included.

Some of the women are quoted at length, making this article one of the few records of the experience of being a lady undertaker in Texas at that time from the perspective of the women themselves. Their insights into the profession are fascinating and illuminating.

The *San Antonio Express* was the second Texas paper to run the syndicated article on some of the state's women undertakers. It dedicated a full page to the piece and included this elaborate headline, including photos of five of the women profiled. *From the* San Antonio Express.

While this is a small sample size, the women who gave explanations for how they ended up in the funeral business all point to their husband as the reason. Ella Fall, who was elected second vice-president of the Undertakers Association the same year the article ran, had watched her husband work as an undertaker for years. Then she became a widow. She said, "I really continued in the business because I did not know any other way that I could invest my money in a better paying business. Of course, I did not know many of the details of the business, but I just determined to go ahead with it, just like Mr. Fall had. So far, I have been more than pleased with the results."

The woman the article identifies as Mrs. Jack Taylor (unfortunately, her own name has proved elusive) suffered even more loss. She, too, was the widow of an undertaker who kept the business going. She said, "I always liked the work. Mr. Taylor had died just two years before, leaving just my baby and me. Then, when the little girl was taken, I had to find some work to keep my mind from thinking of my loss."

As the article points out, more than half the women undertakers (at least, the ones the reporter knew of) were located in sparsely populated West Texas. This was the reason Lucy Thomas gave for how she started in the profession, explaining, "My husband was in the undertaking business, and since they lived so far in the western part of Texas reliable help was hard to find."

Of course, there were also financial considerations, as Ottilie Baumgarten put bluntly: "As a rule we are better paid than in any other line."

While Lucy Thomas originally learned the business from her husband, she later went to the embalming college in Dallas. Her experience there, while wrapped in a cute story, puts in stark relief how outnumbered women were and what they were up against. She remembered, "Not only did I take my course in undertaking there, what I learned while there that none of us need be afraid of that '13' hoodoo. 12 men and I formed the class. Many times, jokes about the number were made. Since I was the only woman in the class the members would jestingly tell me that this was a sure sign that I never would succeed as a sure-enough undertaker. Of course, I did not take this seriously, still for the first few patients I had after returning home I would recall this. My work has been anything but a 'hoodoo,' however."

The women interviewed for the article did not mince words when it came to how hard their career choice could be at times. Lucy Thomas said, "Even though I may get tired out from loss of sleep or from heavy work, still I enjoy it so much that I am always willing to work hard. Not often do I become fatigued."

This stark image of Old La Plata Cemetery in Hereford, Deaf Smith County, pictured in 1896, gives an idea of why lady undertakers in less populated areas like West Texas and the Panhandle had very different career experiences from those in East Texas and large cities. *Deaf Smith County Library.*

It's hard to believe that Ottilie Baumgarten wasn't indulging in hyperbole when she said, "Many times, I have driven 50 or 60 miles in a sandstorm. Some of the time I would have a driver, while again there was nothing left for me to do but make the trip alone." However, she repeated this a second time, so it's clear this event must have happened at least once, and clearly affected her. She explained, "A woman [undertaker] must possess tact, energy and good health. Let me emphatically say to any other women who might consider taking up the work…it is hard and the hours are irregular. I have lost many a night's sleep, working hard all of the next day, and soon after retiring the second night, be called before morning. I have been called in the midst of night to a railroad yard to take charge of what was once some mother's pride. Or, again, drive 50 or 60 miles in a sandstorm to get to some ranch home."

Ottilie Baumgarten was hardly the only one of the women with a horror story though. Lucinda Wheeler told of one particularly bad case:

> *I was called to take charge of a young man's body who had hanged himself in a pumping plant engine room, on a rice farm, about 5 miles from El*

Campo. When I reached the plant body had been taken down and men on the farm had worked with the body, hoping to revive him. No suspicion was given that he had died from anything other than strangulation.

About four hours after death Mr. Wheeler and I began working on the body, which had been brought into our morgue. I proceeded as usual until I began to inject the arteries and began to smell elders of gasoline. I injected perhaps a quart, when water began to lose from the body and stand in large drops as in perspiration.

We finished with the work, but the next day I saw Mr. Wheeler was not satisfied with the work. We opened up the cavities by tracar and gasoline was pumped from the stomach. There must have been at least a quart of this, which proved to us that the man must have drunk gasoline before strangulation.

Fortunately for me, Mr. Wheeler was at home when this happened, but if I had been alone the case would have been very difficult to have handled. That's why a woman undertaker has to face realities as they are. Certainly, in this work, as in no other, many serious problems are to be confronted.

Despite experiences like these, across the board, the women who were quoted emphatically believed that women not only could and should be undertakers but also were a vital part of the funeral business. Ella Fall said, "I find that a woman can manage this business with just as much ease and confidence as she could in any other line, and perhaps far easier than many others."

Of course, even if women in general should consider a career in undertaking, as Ottilie Baumgarten pointed out, it did also come down to the abilities and personality of the individual woman: "If a woman has the physical strength to do all of this, the ability to go into a grief-stricken house, out of confusion and chaos to bring order, to forestall any emergencies that may arise, surely the work is intended for woman." Mrs. Jack Taylor, however, thought that all women had this fortitude, considering what they already dealt with in their everyday lives—

TWENTY-THREE GET LICENSES AS EMBALMERS

Three Women Among Successful Candidates in Examination by State Board.

Despite the encouragement of those already in the business, women were slow to enter the world of undertaking. In 1915, three years after the syndicated newspaper profile appeared, only three women took the exam and received their embalming licenses at the state convention. *From the* Fort Worth Star-Telegram.

An undated photo of lady undertaker Ella Fall with her father, John K. Wemple, "at summer camp in Bosque near Waco," per the inscription on the back. *University of North Texas Libraries/ private collection of T.B. Willis.*

without pay. "A woman is an adaptable creature and understands all of the situations as she meets them. Perhaps on this account do I wish that more women would think seriously of taking up this line. Why, in their daily work they also lend much foam to the 18 hearts, and once retired at night can feel that really they have done some good in the world besides making a living for themselves," she said.

Bettie Lattner, who had more experience that almost any woman undertaker in Texas at that time, made her thoughts on the matter plain, saying, "Not only do I believe in women undertakers, but I firmly think that the time is right here when women will direct funerals as men do. Heretofore women have prepared the bodies for burial and the men have had charge of the funerals. I really think that this day is rapidly on the decline. There are so many things that a woman can do on entering a death chamber that a man never thinks of. Frequently the dresses or groups need a few stitches, and a woman can take these up in a few minutes. Particularly is this true, too, in the arranging of the hair. Men are absolutely lost when it comes to adjusting rats or curls, while a woman knows how they should be. She also knows which is the more becoming way to dress the hair."

But regardless of how these women got into the funeral business or the newspaper-friendly reasons they gave for why the public should accept them as part of that business, at the end of the day, they were undertakers because they enjoyed it. "I do think that it is one of the most interesting [jobs] in the world," Ella Fall said.

HISTORICAL ERASURE

While it's clear that women were entering the funeral business in ever larger numbers during this period, determining if a woman was an undertaker, especially before embalming licenses became a requirement, can be difficult because of the historical erasure of many working women. For decades, many women (or their husbands or perhaps even the census taker) listed "none" under the career column on the U.S. census.

Irma Griggs is a perfect example of the phenomenon, and at the most modern end of this survey at that. She received her embalming degree from the Dallas College of Embalming in 1923 and was listed as an embalmer in the annual Amarillo City Directory throughout the second half of the 1920s. The N.S. Griggs undertaking establishment advertised her as the only licensed woman embalmer in the entire Panhandle in 1929. Yet the 1930 census records her occupation as "none."

Similarly, "housewife" is often the designation given on a lady undertaker's death certificate, either because they were retired by that point or because their domestic work was considered their primary responsibility. Even the obituaries of women for whom there is copious evidence they were active undertakers for years, if not decades, sometimes fail to mention her vocation or simply refer to the deceased as the "wife of" a male undertaker.

Another issue unique to the women in the undertaking business is that some of the work they did was still considered enough in the domestic sphere that it could be easily ignored. In the 1920s, Thelma Hurley, for example, sewed the burial suits for the bodies in the care of her and her husband and even baked chocolate cakes for the bereaved families, according to the modern Hurley Funeral Home and Crematory in Pleasanton. But such work was not the kind that would be included on official forms as an actual "job." It was just the sort of thing that women, all women, were meant to do regardless.

THE BUTT OF THE JOKE

The syndicated 1912 article about Texas's women undertakers received mentions some in newspapers that chose not to run even a truncated version of the original piece. Instead, some simply ran jokes based on the headline alone. (Once again, the headline was wrong even based on the number of women included in the article itself.)

From the August 3, 1912 *Province* newspaper of Vancouver, Canada: "Texas has 13 women undertakers. The cheerful manner in which they conduct the obsequies of old bachelors is a great consolation to the mourners."[92]

From the July 23, 1912 *Wilmington Dispatch*: "Texas has thirteen women undertakers. Verily, thirteen is an unlucky number; in this case being a sign of death."[93]

The barbs about lady undertakers were not limited to Texas. The combination of the easy jokes about women and easy jokes about the undertaking profession proved irresistible for newspaper editors who needed to fill a few empty lines on a page.

This was a format that allowed readers a slight chuckle over breakfast for decades. However, it also helps trace how the idea of a woman undertaker became less shocking over time. The *Lima News* of Ohio mentioned on March 23, 1894, that "Holgate, a village a few miles north of this place on the Clover Leaf,

A 1925 cigarette card from the British game Happy Families, similar to Go Fish, illustrates Mrs. Gasper as a sour caricature of an undertaker's wife. The image of women in the funeral industry as ghoulish and indulging in vice—like smoking or drinking—was one that dated back to the days of the shrouding women. *New York Public Library.*

enjoys a luxury that is very rare—a lady undertaker." Forty-five years later, in 1939, *Gone with the Wind* author Margaret Mitchell, who was at the height of her fame that year with the release of the film version of her book, wrote to a friend, "[It was a] heartening fact that people no longer treated me a curiosity but took me for granted just as if I had been a successful lady embalmer or life insurance salesman." It might have taken half a century, but women undertakers had gone from "very rare" to "[taken] for granted."

While patiently waiting for the change to happen, though, lady undertakers had to put up with the terrible jokes. There were so many, in fact, and newspaper editors were seemingly so bad at coming up with new jokes on their own, that patterns emerged and jokes were recycled for years. Take, for example, a single lady undertaker of Smith Centre, Kansas, who apparently blew the minds of reporters in the state so completely that they could not come up with good jokes about her, although that did not keep them from trying.

From the February 18, 1892 *Glen Elder Sentinel* (Kansas): "Smith Centre had a lady undertaker which is the only one in the state—A lady undertaker might be all right after one is dead, but somehow—Oh, well, let's change the subject."

From the February 18, 1892 *Osborne County Farmer* (Kansas): "Smith Center has a lady undertaker, and some of the susceptible men of that town are longing for a chance to die."

From the September 28, 1900 *Council Grove Republican* (Kansas): "Women are getting into almost every line of business. Smith Center has a lady undertaker who advertises to plant people with neatness and dispatch."

Perhaps the weirdest and most uncomfortable genre of lady undertaker joke were the ones that implied, even vaguely, of something sexual or romantic about the idea of a woman undertaker and a male corpse. Despite its questionable taste, this was seemingly the most common punchline to lady undertaker jokes.

From the September 14, 1893 *Cornishman* newspaper of England: "A Boston woman is a licensed undertaker. One of the nicest things to have about, from the cradle to the grave, is a winsome, kindly-disposed woman. The man is a churl who wouldn't let a pretty lady-undertaker embalm him."

From the July 18, 1894 *Daily Globe* (Kansas): "St. Joe has a young lady embalmer. But it doesn't make death any easier for the men to know that a woman will lay them out, and squirt embalming fluid into them."

From the July 19, 1895 *Arkansas City Daily Traveler* (Kansas): "Lady undertakers is an eastern fad that we hope will not extend into the west. A great many men would rib up some kind of excuse in order to die so that they could be embalmed by a woman. Anyway, why shouldn't a woman be an undertaker."

MISS GASPER

THE UNDERTAKER'S DAUGHTER

Many women learned the undertaking business from their parents or ran a funeral home alongside a brother or sister. The 1925 Happy Families cigarette card collection did not pull its punches when it came to the girls and women who grew up among the dead. *New York Public Library.*

From the August 28, 1897 *Leicester Chronicle and Leicestershire Mercury* (England): "[A] lady advertises that she is prepared to undertake all kinds of funerals in a sympathetic spirit and at the lowest possible prices. The knowledge that the last details of a man's earthly career will be lovingly cared for by a female undertaker must reconcile many to the supreme ordeal, and only confirmed, unreasoning misogynists could long resist her blandishments."

From the July 18, 1901 *Nickerson Argosy* (Kansas): "Sterling has a lady undertaker. It may prove a blessing to die in that town and be embalmed by a lady undertaker."

ABREAST OF THE TIMES·

ONE by one the lingering shadows of the dark ages are disappearing from the present century, and many customs which prejudice long rendered inviolable are being abandoned. The full daylight of progress has taken possession of the court, the school and the pulpit, while even the undertaker no longer invites to somber, gruesome halls of death. Loving relatives and friends assemble instead in a place more befitting the last obsequies of the loved one whose spirit has passed to a lovely hereafter. Why should the last view ever be a reminder of what the loved one did not look like in life? Why leave reason to dread that last look when skillful hands can so easily transform the loved one into the semblance of one who is but sleeping?

Every reform or progressive idea nevertheless requires a leader, and fortunately at least one Los Angeles undertaking establishment has shown itself fully abreast of the non-progressive East by adding to the many advantages of their establishment a department which every reader will agree fills a great need.

It is certainly as consistent, and should be as compulsory, for every establishment to include in its personnel a lady embalmer and attendant as representatives of the opposite sex. When, therefore, an establishment is so far ahead of local progress that it furnishes the public not merely a female assistant, but a leader in that department, who is in every sense an artist and inventor, whose sympathetic instincts and ability render that department almost an innovation in the right direction, the fact becomes one of great public interest.

The *Arkansas City Daily Traveler* may have hoped that lady undertakers would stay back east, but just four years later, in 1899, it was clear that women were involved in the funeral business as far west as they could get in the contiguous United States. This two-page ad appeared in *Out West* magazine, with a dozen illustrious Californians singing the praises of Mrs. Madge Connell of Los Angeles. *Author's collection.*

From the September 1921 *Steam Shovel and Dredge* (vol. 30, no. 3): "Why Wait? As a special inducement to kick the bucket a Yonkers undertaker advertised an artistic 'Lady Embalmer.'"

Then there were the jokes with an edge, the ones that implied women should not be undertakers at all, or in any jobs, that were the domain of men.

From the February 3, 1892 *Pacific Bee* (California): "An undertaker in San Francisco advertises that he has 'lady undertakers' to prepare 'lady corpses' for the grave. We wonder if the Almighty has fallen into the new fad and will have 'lady angels' to usher these 'lady corpses' into 'lady heaven?' Bah! The very sight of the name sickens a man, and certainly ought to nauseate every true woman."

From the December 21, 1903 *St. Joseph News-Press* (Missouri): "Spokane, Washington, has a 'lady undertaker.' Guess De Hillis was right when he said the women would overtake the men in fifty years—only he put it off entirely too long."

REVERSE SEXISM

While the jokes about women undertakers were popular, the reality was that so was the availability of lady undertakers in a community. In fact, eventually they were a must, so much so that small towns would put ads in the newspapers of major metropolises searching for women undertakers, or at least men undertakers with lady assistants, hoping to entice them to move there.

From the February 21, 1915 *San Antonio Express*: "Undertaking business consisting of hearse, wagon and stock of goods in South Texas town of 5,000 population. Not much cash required to handle. Good chance for embalmer with lady assistant."

From the February 24, 1929 *Fort Worth Star-Telegram*: "Wanted—Splendid opportunity for experienced lady embalmer and undertaker in thriving oil and railroad town of 12,000; must be up to date, of high principles and must stand investigation."

At its core, the rationale for and eventual necessity of women undertakers was really about a kind of reverse sexism. Women in the funeral business were often, if not usually, advertised as "lady attendants" or "lady assistants," regardless of how experienced they were or if they were an equal partner in the business. Advertisements for funeral homes routinely noted that the women on staff were there to care for the bodies of women and children. Like the jokes about men being more willing to die if a pretty lady undertaker would be the one embalming them, there was a strange undercurrent to this reasoning; what was unsaid—barely—was that somehow a male undertaker seeing a dead woman naked and handling her body was inappropriate.

J.E. Nagley, speaking to the *El Paso Times* in 1899, explained the benefits of having his wife, Minnie Nagley, on the staff of his new undertaking establishment: "Another thing entirely new to the city will be that deceased women and children will be cared for by a lady undertaker. A great many people naturally prefer that the female deceased friends and relatives would be in charge of a lady."

It was uncommon for newspapers to name a specific person who embalmed a body, sticking to the name of the business or the proprietor in most cases, but there were exceptions. For example, in 1915, the year Emma Parker earned her embalming license, the *Weekly Democrat-Gazette* reported that she prepared the bodies of both a thirty-two-year-old woman and a forty-year-old woman within a week of each other in August.

Because the embalmers were not usually specified in death announcements, it's difficult to know if women embalmed male corpses more often than

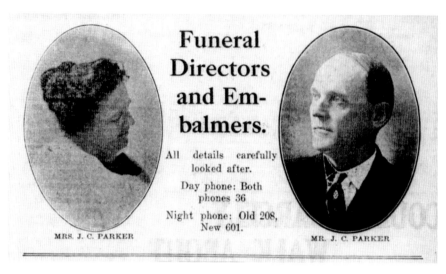

Emma Parker earned her embalming license in 1915. Her name and image were used liberally in both advertisements and newspaper articles, visually placing her equal in importance with her husband. *From the* Courier-Gazette.

funeral home advertisements would have one think. Were the "jokes" about the inappropriateness of women embalming men based in real feeling, or was it only men embalming women that society found unacceptable? One example of a lady undertaker being mentioned by name was when the *Laredo Weekly Times* reported Olivia Schwartz had embalmed an adult man, a train engineer who was murdered in Baird in 1913.

Tragic Women

As women undertakers were pitched as the only appropriate people to take care of the bodies of women and children, this logically followed that many of the most tragic deaths fell to them to deal with.

One horrific pattern was the murder of women by their husbands, often in a violent murder-suicide. Annie Ross in 1892, Caroline McCulloch in 1902 and Lorena Brulin in 1926 all took charge of the bodies of women who were killed by their husbands or other romantic partners before the man killed himself.

While most of these tragic crimes involved firearms, in 1920, A.D. Payne purposely blew up himself and his wife with a bomb. Amazingly, almost all his funeral wishes were followed by Irene Boxwell's establishment; she even

OUR BELOVED DAUGHTER
TERESA M. FOSSATI
BORN APRIL 5,1887
DIED SEPT. 9,1905
GONE, BUT NOT FORGOTTEN.

FOSSATI

While early childhood was the most dangerous time, young adults were also at an increased chance of death before the advent of modern medicine. Many, like eighteen-year-old Teresa M. Fossati of Victoria, slowly got sicker and sicker over several months until they finally died. The announcement of her death reported that she was "suffering greatly" and that her last words were "Papa and Mama, I have got to die; don't worry." *J.D. Mitchell/Victoria College/University of Houston-Victoria Library.*

sang his selected a hymn at the ceremony. The only request that was ignored was his desire to be buried with the wife he murdered. An estimated ten thousand people viewed the casket, and one thousand went to the funeral. The president of his former school called the murderer a "perfect student and as near a perfect citizen as the town ever had,"[94] which takes saying only nice things about the dead to quite another level.

Women undertakers were also tasked with preparing the bodies of women, particularly young women it seems, who died by suicide. Queen East took charge of the remains of someone whom the *Cooper Review* moralized was a "fallen woman"[95] whose allegedly bad choices had led to her fate in 1912. Another young woman, who'd died by suicide from carbolic acid poisoning in 1908, had her remains brought to Annie Ludwig's parlor.

When word got out that Lola Westheimer's funeral home was displaying the body of yet another young woman who died by suicide in 1912, hundreds of women and girls came to see her corpse. The *Houston Post* reported that "an almost unbroken stream of womankind filed in and out the small room that had been temporarily improvised into a public morgue....It was stated by the undertakers in charge that never in the history of the establishment have so many people, particularly women and girls of the varied classes, ages and stations in life represented, entered that place in a single day."[96]

Tragic Children

At a period when infant mortality rates were astronomically higher than they are today, embalming or arranging the bodies of children was a seemingly never-ending painful task for early women undertakers in Texas. Obituaries were often vague about what caused the deaths of infants, although it's possible there was no way to tell.

Following are just some of the many deaths of infants and toddlers that lady undertakers were faced with:

Annie Ross
1898: baby died after sickness
1899: baby given up by its mother and then died, no reason given

Anna Beck
1915: nineteen-month-old boy, no reason given

Flossie Dannel
1917: infant child, no reason given

Bertha Allen
1919: "little infant,"[97] no reason given
1921: sixteen-month-old, no reason given
1923: eighteen-month-old, no reason given

Lennora Weadock
1921: six-month-old who had been in a sanitarium, no reason given

Mildred McKinney
1922: six-month and twenty-two-day-old, no reason given

Ada Hatchell
1929: one-week-old baby, no reason given

Angela Guillen
1929: one-year-old, no reason given

Lottie Johnston
1930: infant, no reason given

While most babies the women undertakers prepared for burial died natural deaths at home, in a time when not every pregnancy was considered acceptable and a newborn was difficult to hide, some women took the drastic step of abandoning their infants. When a baby was discovered dead in a bag in 1924, the body was taken to Flossie Dannel's funeral parlor, while the mother was tracked down and arrested. Hattie Faircloth took charge of the remains of an infant found in some bushes in 1923. And in 1913, children playing by a river stumbled across the body of a dead newborn. The child was buried by Elizabeth Denning's establishment.

Surviving infancy meant the most dangerous time was behind them, but children still risked death every day; some of them were taken from the world far too soon.

Willie Horner's funeral parlor took charge of the body of a four-year-old boy whom the *El Paso Herald* reported had died of "laryngitis" in 1906.[98] As the diagnosis is never fatal, it's unclear what the young boy's actual cause of death was.

Mrs. Lizzie Crosson
Born Aug. 25, 1844.
Died Nov. 17, 1924.
Age 80 yrs. 2 mos. 22 D.

We miss thee from our home, dear mother,
We miss thee from thy place,
A shadow o'er our life is cast,
We miss the sunshine of thy face.
We miss thy kind and willing hand,
Thy fond and earnest care,
Our home is dark without thee—
We miss thee everywhere.

IN LOVING REMEMBRANCE

While child mortality was far higher then than it is now, plenty of people in the period lived to a very old age, like Lizzie Crosson of Marfa, who passed her eightieth birthday. *Marfa Public Library.*

Mabel Ratliff was around fourteen years old when she died "after a long illness" in 1921.[99] Ida Dawson's parlor prepared the girl's body, and the high school she attended sent a large and expensive floral arrangement for her funeral.

Lady undertakers also grappled with some of the most tragic accidental deaths imaginable. In 1902, Bishop Glass, only nine years old, drowned in the Colorado River. The *Austin American-Statesman* reported that just minutes before the boy found himself in distress, he reassured his concerned mother, "Mamma, you need not be uneasy about me being drowned; I have been bathing lots of times."[100] There was a long search for his body, with the party including Rush McCulloch, husband of lady undertaker Caroline McCulloch. The couple took charge of the body after the boy was found.

In 1913, sixteen-year-old Walter Lorance got into a fight at school, and the other boy, who was a friend, stabbed him in the head. Lorance lingered for four long months before dying from "compression of the brain" as a result of the stabbing.[101] Elizabeth Denning's parlor in San Angelo prepared the body for shipment to Bronte.

Anna Mary Beetham's parlor prepared the body of the victim of a freak accident, seventeen-year-old Katherine Jennings, a Pennsylvania native who was visiting Mineral Wells with her family in 1918 and staying at the famous Crazy Hotel. After attending a dance, she returned to the family's fourth-floor room. Then tragedy struck out of nowhere, as the *Graham Leader* reported: "After retiring to their apartments her mother asked her to lower the shade and to do this she stood upon a small desk, which was a little to one side of the window, and as she reached for the shade, the desk tilted and she fell backward, helplessly carrying the screen with her to the sidewalk."[102] She died about forty-five minutes after the accident.

To attempt to get one's mind around what preparing the corpses of infants and children day in and day out would be like, one has only to look at Alma

A photo of "The Sllew La Renim Club" (Mineral Wells spelled backward), circa 1912–14. Anna Mary Beetham's daughter Emma is pictured at the far right. Born in 1888, as Emma grew up, some of the children and young women her mother prepared for burial would undoubtedly have reminded her of her daughter, as well as the three children she herself had lost. *Boyce Ditto Public Library.*

Johnson and some of the cases in charge of Johnson's Funeral Home of San Angelo across five months of 1929 (dates are when the children's obituaries appeared in the newspaper):

- June 20: three-day-old girl, no reason given
- July 17: thirteen-day-old infant, parents lived in tent
- August 21: three-year-old boy, after an operation for appendicitis
- October 25: four-month-old, after getting "treatment" for an unspecified issue for a week[103]
- November 1: eleven-year-old girl, typhoid after being sick for three weeks
- November 4: four-month-old boy, no reason given
- November 25: four-year-old "Mexican boy," no reason given

When you are dealing with the deaths of so many children in a relatively small population in such a short period, it becomes clear just how important the role of a lady undertaker was to a community. If the societal biases of the times meant that parents would find a small amount of comfort knowing a woman was preparing their child for burial, then having a trained lady undertaker available was both right and necessary.

Yet, ironically, due to those same core beliefs about what role a woman should play in society, there were plenty who would have preferred to see no lady undertakers in business at all. In 1912, Mrs. Gilbert Jones, a leader of the anti-suffrage movement, explained why she was against not just women voting but also women working in specific fields: "As woman is forced out of her home and away from motherhood, into extreme social, industrial and political life, just so must she pay the price of her emancipation by the tax on her physical and moral strength....Some women are equal to this strain, but the majority are not, and we should look for fewer women wage earners.... Discourage women blacksmiths, baggage masters and women brakemen and women undertakers."[104]

RACISM

Reconstruction ended on March 31, 1877, and the first known use of the phrase "Jim Crow law" came in 1884. In the South, including Texas, the biases, unequal treatment and divide between the Black and white communities—both legal and societal—were unavoidable in the funeral industry.

Ida Dawson and her husband, J.J. Dawson, lived in Temple, Texas, until 1920, when they moved to Oklahoma City. Ida was the lady attendant that their new funeral home there advertised as a "unique service" in 1921. *From the* Black Dispatch.

Black male undertakers tended to be important men in their communities, while still facing racism from white Texans. Adlanta Guest and her husband were exceptionally successful in the funeral business. George Guest was born into enslavement at the very end of the Civil War and left an astonishing $100,000 estate when he died in 1948.

Black women faced double the prejudice, although they also could achieve some sort of condescending acceptance through running a successful funeral parlor. When Narcissa Horton and Katie Lee Childs died in 1935 and 1938, respectively, their deaths both received short write-ups in their local white newspapers. While Horton was described as a "colored woman undertaker" and Childs as a "well-known negress," the fact that their deaths merited mention in the white community indicates how important these Black women and their businesses were in their cities.

Just as a white newspaper acknowledging a Black death was a backhanded compliment to the deceased, so too did white reporters note with importance when white men and women attended the funeral of a Black person. When Adlanta Guest buried Julia Alexandra, half of one of the wealthiest Black couples in North Texas, in 1918, more than one thousand people attended her funeral in Bairdstown. The *Paris Morning News* reported that this large crowd included "several white acquaintances." When the white

Lucy Laughter's undertaking establishment buried Lucy Merrell in 1927, the article covering the funeral in the *Abilene Reporter-News* used astonishing language, calling Merrell "Mammy," praising her "devotion—that of an old Southern negro to her master" and saying that she died of grief after the white man for whom she'd worked since she was ten years old passed away. It also noted that more than one hundred people came to her funeral, and only one of them was Black.

One reason the attendance of white mourners at the funeral of a Black person was notable was that funerals in Texas in this period were almost always held along racial lines. Black corpses were buried by Black undertakers, often in cemeteries set aside for those Black bodies, in order that white cemeteries were kept white. In some cases, the racial lines were literal, like at Greenwood Cemetery in Waco, which had a fence dividing the white and Black sides of the burial ground until 2016.

Sometimes even this division was not enough. In 1911, the *Fort Worth Record and Register* reported that some lots near the train tracks in Frisco had "recently come into the hands of the negros"—in other words, they legally purchased them—and the new owners, including an undertaker, planned to start a Black cemetery there. There should have been no issue with this since a white cemetery already bordered that location. But the proximity was an issue for the white community, and the city government adopted a new ordinance that was specifically intended to make their project impossible.

Louise Perry's establishment, like many funeral homes, offered an ambulance service; however, as the company made clear in its advertisements in 1913, the ambulance was available to whites only.

There were some white funeral directors who were, at the very least, not that blatantly unwelcoming to Black customers. In 1905, the undertaking establishment of Nannie Taliaferro and her husband, then located in Oklahoma, as they would not move to Texas until 1909, was included on a list in the *Baptist Rival* of white business owners who were "not prejudiced… and are well disposed towards colored people who have self-respect." The paper urged its readers to "spend your money with those men."

When Minnie Stickley and her husband were interviewed about their lives and career in 1950, the journalist asked them if they had ever buried any Black people. A shocking question, to which they, shockingly, had a ready answer: "Only two. One was a Negro who was killed on the railroad. The other was old Topsy, a figure almost legendary now, but that of a Negro man who was a bartender in a saloon in Canadian in the old days."[105]

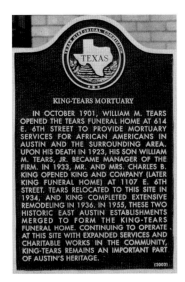

KING-TEARS MORTUARY

IN OCTOBER 1901, WILLIAM M. TEARS OPENED THE TEARS FUNERAL HOME AT 614 E. 6TH STREET TO PROVIDE MORTUARY SERVICES FOR AFRICAN AMERICANS IN AUSTIN AND THE SURROUNDING AREA. UPON HIS DEATH IN 1923, HIS SON WILLIAM M. TEARS, JR. BECAME MANAGER OF THE FIRM. IN 1933, MR. AND MRS. CHARLES B. KING OPENED KING AND COMPANY (LATER KING FUNERAL HOME) AT 1107 E. 6TH STREET. TEARS RELOCATED TO THIS SITE IN 1934, AND KING COMPLETED EXTENSIVE REMODELING IN 1936. IN 1955, THESE TWO HISTORIC EAST AUSTIN ESTABLISHMENTS MERGED TO FORM THE KING-TEARS FUNERAL HOME. CONTINUING TO OPERATE AT THIS SITE WITH EXPANDED SERVICES AND CHARITABLE WORKS IN THE COMMUNITY, KING-TEARS REMAINS AN IMPORTANT PART OF AUSTIN'S HERITAGE.

(2002)

As Texas Historical Commission Marker no. 12826 records, Black-owned funeral homes like that of William M. Tears in Austin were necessary "to provide mortuary services for African Americans," as many white undertakers would not agree to prepare or bury Black bodies. *Keith Peterson/Historical Marker Database.*

When the records of the Dannel Funeral Home in Sherman, owned by Illinois natives Flossie Dannel and her husband, John Carlton Dannel, were examined for *Celebrating 100 Years of the Texas Folklore Society, 1909–2009* by Jerry B. Lincecum, he discovered that the white undertakers had buried fourteen Black men and women in 1909. This was especially notable because Sherman had a Black-owned undertaking establishment as well.

Isabel Sutherland's husband, Christopher "Bank" Sutherland, was a big name in the Texas funeral industry, including as one of the thirty founding members of the state undertakers' association and a member of the embalming board. His 1928 obituary was a front-page story in the *Corsicana Daily Sun* and included this anecdote: "Mr. Sutherland never would allow a white woman to be buried in the 'potter's field' and when a body was left with no one to look after it or care what disposition was made of it, he would have it interred in another cemetery, at his own expense. He said on a number of occasions that he could not bear to see a white woman buried in the 'potter's field.'"[106]

While paying for the funerals of those who cannot afford them is honorable—above and beyond the responsibilities of his vocation—and a man feeling that he should do this for women fit with the chivalrous ideas of the time, it is impossible to not cringe at the specificity of "white women." This means that he *did* allow Black women to be buried as paupers, as if they were less deserving of honor in death than white women.

All of this bias and racism faced Maggie Fulleylove Starks when she found herself a twenty-two-year-old widow with a young child. She decided to return home and attempt a career in which she had no experience in order to help her community: "At the time, there were no negro undertakers in San Angelo, and I felt I could serve my people out here. I wanted to be my own boss."

She made a huge success of the business. The respect her fellow undertakers had for her was clearly evident when Jim Crow laws were made illegal and desegregation was enforced starting in the second half of the 1950s. This meant that Black families could choose to bring their dead to white parlors for what was effectively the first time in many parts of Texas. When this happened for the first time at Johnson's Funeral Home—the parlor of Alma Johnson—Starks received a phone call from her competition. He made it clear to her that Johnson's did not want the job—not because the deceased was Black, but because he knew he was taking a job that previously would have been hers. "Maggie, I hate to do this, but if we refuse, we could be sued." The Massie business expressed similar sentiments. She told them not to worry: "The Blacks put me where I am today....I said, 'You go on and bury them; I will make it.'" And she did.

Part III

THE PERSONAL

Undertaking in Texas, 1920–1929

If 1900 saw Texas undertaking become a business, 1920 was when it became an industry. Over the next decade, that industry modernized at an astonishing speed.

1920
While the May 19 edition of the *Waco News Tribune* reported on page one that the members of the Texas Undertakers and Embalmers' Association were in town attending their annual convention "with their wives," on page nine, it did allow that "six of the twenty"[107] women embalmers in the state were there as well. "So far as [is] known," this year also saw the first time embalming fluid was shipped by airplane.[108]

1921
The National Funeral Directors Association held its annual convention in Texas for the first time.

The program at the national convention hints at cracks in the funeral business. No longer the vital personage of a community who could deal with corpses, it is clear that the public now saw undertakers as businesspeople who were out for a buck and would cut corners. The delegates discussed how to raise standards in their profession and also "adopted a report which asserted that the press, pulpit and magazines are continually directing unfair criticism toward undertakers."[109]

39ᵗʰ Annual Convention of Texas Funer

The 39th Annual Convention of Texas Funeral Directors Association took place in Austin in 1925. It was a particularly important year for the organization, and the first female governor of Texas, Miriam A. "Ma" Ferguson, gave a speech. While at least fourteen women are visible in this group photo, just one took the embalmers exam that year. *Austin History Center, Austin Public Library.*

Nor were the many complaints about the high cost of funerals the fault of the undertakers, since "the low mortality rate in the United States, combined with the high overhead of manufacturers of the country, made cheaper burial impossible,"[110] according to Hal Miller, chairman of the national association's committee on prices.

1922
State Health Officer Dr. J.H. Florence spoke to the convention and threatened the undertakers with prosecution if they did not file death certificates with the state on a more consistent basis.

1923
While attending the annual convention in Fort Worth, R.H. Leatherwood, president of the association—and husband of lady undertaker Minnie Leatherwood—gave a radio address in which he "explained the advancement of his profession from obscurity to a much respected institution in the past forty years."[111]

1924
A speaker at the Texas convention in Dallas opined that *undertaker* was an obsolete word now that embalming had been perfected.

ASSOCIATION – AUSTIN, TEXAS – MAY 19-21, 1925.

1925

The national association pushed vocabulary changes, objecting to the terms *undertaker, hearse* and *coffin* as old-fashioned. They recommended using instead *mortuary, funeral car* and *casket.*

Governor Miriam A. "Ma" Ferguson, the first woman governor of Texas, addressed the convention. However, women more generally were not well represented that year, as the *Austin American* reported that only one "white woman"[112] took the embalming exam, and she wasn't even from Texas.

Speakers explained how the modern mortuary was no longer a "chamber of horrors,"[113] which meant that the "secrecy now attending the funeral directors' business should be removed."[114]

1926

The Colored Funeral Directors Association of Texas incorporates, twenty-three years after Black undertakers first organized in the state.

1927

The new version of the Colored Funeral Directors Association held its first convention in El Paso. It took place at the same time as the white Texas Funeral Directors Association in the same city, and the latter body's president, T.S. Wright (husband of lady undertaker Charlie Wright), spoke at the former's convention. However, this served to highlight that the two were completely separate entities divided by the color line.

INTERVIEWS WITH ATTENDEES AT the Texas association's annual conferences during the 1920s emphasized the *change* to the funeral business. The undertakers of the late nineteenth century and even the first decade and a half of the twentieth century had, essentially, done things wrong. They had only primitive methods to work with and were not as large and successful as the cutting-edge mortuaries of the 1920s.

A 1922 profile of Charles Weiland (husband of lady undertaker Cora Weiland) and his Dallas establishment bragged that after "[s]tarting in a most unpropitious way with a hole in the wall as an office, and a one horse shay as a hearse, the Weiland Undertaking Company has had a most prodigious growth."[115] That same attitude applied to the industry as a whole.

At the 1926 convention, a reporter for the *Fort Worth Star-Telegram* spoke to Arthur Woodward, described as the "owner of a big motor livery establishment" in the city. Woodward painted a detailed picture of the funeral of old, when he was merely a "hack driver," and the paper printed a paraphrased version of his remembrances:

> *The memory of a funeral 50 years ago in Fort Worth—on a hot day…*
>
> *Time: 1 p.m.—Grief at the home where the body has lain for one, two, or three days. Sobbing women wearing heavy black veils that trail the ground and cover their faces to a point of suffocation. Black hearse, black horses, decorated with black plumes, and the horses with heavy netting.*
>
> *Six pallbearers, the only sign of white being faces, shirt bosoms and gloves, lie up three on each side of the hearse.*
>
> *…The sun pours down.…The slower the march, the more time to mourn.…And at the end of the three weary miles, the open grave. There is no lining in it—just a hole in the ground; no modern machine of easing the coffin down. It has to be slipped on straps held by nearly blistered hands.*
>
> *But, first of all, the casket must be opened for a final look. Women faint and hack horses gallop back to town.*
>
> *There is prayer and a long sermon. Sometimes it's dark before the final clod* [of dirt] *is patted down. Hack drivers light the little oil lamps at each side of the box they sit on. It's cooler as the horses amble homeward a little faster. Returning vehicles, save one, are more crowded.…*
>
> *The modern, motorized funeral by comparison has been likened to painless dentistry.*[116]

Austin delegate W.A. Findley (husband of lady undertaker Dosia Findley) was quoted at length by the *Fort Worth Record-Telegram* when he attended the 1922 convention. He had negative things to say about how those in his business had conducted funerals even as recently as 1907:

> *Fifteen years ago, funerals were not so expensive, but they were much cruder. Because fifteen years ago there were not automobile motor hearses or funeral cars in Austin, and the only mode of transportation utilized by undertakers was the wagon, while horses, buggies and other wagons carried the mourner and pallbearers.*
>
> *Nowadays an undertaker has a beautiful display of coffins and supplies. Before…it was little more than a wooden box. Embalming was practically unheard of fifteen years ago, and where it was practiced the jobs were bungled by inexperienced men.…*
>
> *The modern funeral directors, with his modern facilities, can do ten times the work that the same man could do in 1905 and 1907. And with the modern motor-propelled vehicles he can cover ten times the amount of territory.*[117]

Newspapers written for white audiences explained that Black undertakers were also becoming cutting-edge with their offerings in the 1920s, although the reporters did not interview any Black people to learn this. Instead, they deduced it from the fact that white undertakers were complaining that their Black counterparts would no longer pay big money for the white undertakers' castoffs: "Modern funeral directors sold, for example, the hearse that cost $1,750 for $250 and admit it wouldn't bring $50 now. They go in for motorized vehicles. The negro undertaker, too, is gradually becoming a director."[118]

The decade that saw the discovery of the Tomb of Tutankhamun in Egypt by Howard Carter led to a mania for all things Ancient Egyptian. But according to C.B. Cook, president of the association, when speaking to the convention in 1926, those who had preserved King Tut more than three thousand years earlier could learn a thing or two from modern Texas undertakers: "Today we are able to preserve the features, an art that was unknown to the Egyptians. Bodies embalmed with modern methods will last as long as the mummies found in Egypt and the work is much more perfect."[119]

As undertakers—or rather, funeral directors—became serious businesspeople with accountants and multiple locations and a reactionary attitude to criticism of their industry, the line between professional and personal became more defined. While still a vocation, the funeral industry

This funeral in Fort Worth in August 1920 had classic Texas cowboys as part of the procession, but everything else about it heralded in the rapid change coming in the new decade. Besides the row of funeral cars, the deceased was twenty-eight-year-old silent film star Ormer Locklear, who had died in an airplane crash while attempting a stunt for his next movie. *University of Texas at Dallas.*

was now a career. There was less flow between the life an undertaker led outside their parlor and the business they engaged in inside it. But there was, nonetheless, still a personal side to the women of the profession.

FREE TIME

Not everything about the life of a Texas lady undertaker was depressing, of course. While the caricature of the sour undertaker's wife all in black was popular in fiction and the media, in reality, they were just as joyous as anyone else. The papers of the time were filled with notices that the lady undertakers had hosted a party, returned from visiting family, won handily on bridge night, broken a record in a bowling league, gone for a Sunday drive with an automobile party or joined one of the many fraternal orders that were popular at the time. (This was a period when newspapers were effectively the community's social media page and reported on every little event in the local population's lives.) The reports on the annual Texas Undertakers Association conventions often highlight how fun they were and how ready for a good time the attendees appeared, often to the feigned shock of the journalist writing the piece.

Some of the more unusual stories about their lives deserve mention. In 1911, the *Austin American-Statesman* ran a glowing profile on a member of Lorena Brulin's family. This was Whistler, a "good, ugly, ugly old bulldog with the kind of face that grows on one with acquaintance."[120] He enjoyed watching firemen put out fires, although it was noted that he had never heroically saved anyone from a blaze—yet. He also wore a wooden leg, having lost one when he was run over by a streetcar, and a law firm was planning on suing the company responsible on Whistler's behalf.

Jeanette Fogle and her husband, Ray, also had a pet that was well-known to locals, although in that case, the locals were not at all happy about it. In 1926, the *McAllen Daily Press* reported that the wild monkey that the couple, for some reason, kept as their pet had to be destroyed after it escaped and "terrorized the neighborhood" for four days.[121]

In El Paso, Esther Hagedon spent her free time entering her greyhounds into dog shows. At a large event in 1928, Gaulstown Anna won best in breed.

Employees hanging out outside Truax and Hopkins' Undertaking, Hardware and Furniture Store in Beaver, Oklahoma, circa 1905. *Oklahoma Historical Society.*

Meanwhile, her husband, Barry Hagedon, led an ultimately unsuccessful charge to get the city to adopt Daylight Savings Time.

One year after Amelia Earhart became the first woman to fly solo across the Atlantic Ocean, Dorothy Hogle enrolled in flying school in Wichita Falls.

PERSONAL INJURIES AND ILLNESSES

One of the reasons for the success of many undertaking establishments could also be to the detriment of those involved in running them. Early modern Texas was a dangerous place, with accidents and injuries putting lady undertakers out of commission occasionally. The standard of medicine at the time also meant that medical care could result in a long convalescence. Their respective local newspapers reported that Ottilie Baumgarten was still recovering from burns a month after she was injured in 1899, Louise Perry needed an operation from appendicitis in 1916, Ida Dawson had a "very complicated operation" in 1921, Alma Ryan an unspecified operation in 1922 and Viola Goodson a major operation to fix a stomach abscess in 1930.

Automobiles and other new technologies often led to newspaper-worthy injuries involving lady undertakers or members of their families. While driving her car in Wichita Falls in 1925, Fayne Hines was involved in a collision. She and her husband took the other driver to court, asking for $6,000 in damages for her injuries. After a long deliberation, the jury awarded them $1,000, but Hines was also found partially liable for the accident.

FAMILY INJURIES AND ILLNESSES

Sarah Kinney, her husband and her eleven- and fourteen-year-old sons were all so badly injured in a three-car wreck in 1929 that they were all taken to a hospital by ambulance (an ambulance, incidentally, that was supplied by another funeral home). Viola Goodson's husband suffered several broken ribs in a car accident during icy weather in 1930, while Bess Ella Henderson's husband got off much lighter with only a "very painful" sprained arm he received stepping out of a moving car in 1918. The *Courier-Gazette* of McKinney reported that despite the arm being in a sling, he was still able to work; however, this does illustrate how these injuries, even the

ANNOUNCING
Licensed Lady Embalmer

M. M. Nix & Company are pleased to announce the addition of Mr. and Mrs. C. L. Merritt to their staff.

They have been connected with the Goodson Funeral Home of Wellington in the past. Both are licensed embalmers and have had many years experience.

Enlargement of the staff is another step by M. M. Nix & Company to give Shamrock and vicinity mortuary service that is second to none in the Panhandle.

M. M. Nix & Company
Phone 61____   Funeral Directors   Shamrock

Even as late as 1930, adding a lady embalmer to the staff of a funeral home was deserving of a major advertising campaign, as when Mary Merritt and her husband joined M.M. Nix & Company. *From the* Shamrock Texan.

seemingly minor ones, could mean that a lady undertaker's husband was laid up and unable to help with the business, presumably meaning that the job would be left to her to handle.

When Rush McCullough came down with dengue fever in 1907, it was not just his wife, Caroline McCulloch, who had reason to worry. While the *San Antonio Light* assured its readers that everything was being done to stop the spread of the disease and no one needed to panic, it was clear that McCullough was very ill. While San Antonio was a large enough city to keep several undertaking establishments in business, one can imagine the problem a small, isolated town with just one funeral parlor would face if those running it were too sick to work or even died during a widespread outbreak of disease that left many other bodies in its wake.

In 1905, Willie Horner's husband, C.O. Horner, was unable to work due to a case of blood poisoning, and he even received an insurance payout of almost $100 to cover the "disability."[122]

Mary Merritt's husband, Leonard, who also happened to be the brother of Viola Goodson, had an operation for appendicitis in 1930 that managed to disrupt both couples' undertaking businesses because his sister and brother-in-law came to be with him during his convalescence.

A DEATH IN THE FAMILY

Due to the "women and children" policy of many lady undertakers, it is clear that they dealt with some of the most tragic cases to darken their funeral home's door. Adding to the difficulty of such circumstances was the fact that most of these women were mothers, and of those who were, many had lost children of their own.

The high rate of stillbirths and infant mortality was an unavoidable reality for these women both at work and at home. Viola Goodson delivered a stillborn daughter in 1924. Ella Ebensberger gave birth in 1917, but the newborn boy died after just three hours, too quickly for the parents to give him a name, according to his death certificate.

There were dangers beyond infancy, of course. Out of the five children Anna Mary Beetham gave birth to, three died in early childhood. Louise Perry lost her eight-year-old daughter Louise to diphtheria in 1909. The *Houston Post* reported that the girl was sick for less than a day before she died.

Josefa Estrada's eighteen-month-old daughter, also named Josefa, was playing in the road in 1902 when she was crushed by a grocery wagon. While witnesses agreed that it was a terrible accident that couldn't have been avoided and the driver was later found blameless at an inquest, the child's parents were obviously distraught. When he learned about the tragedy, the little girl's father grabbed a gun, declaring that he was going to kill the driver, but he was stopped by friends before he could do something he would regret. The child's body was prepared by the undertaking establishment Nagley & Carr, which employed both the Estradas, as well as Minnie Nagley.

Caroline McCulloch faced a mother's worst nightmare in 1903 when her baby son fell out of bed and suffered a bad head injury, but thankfully, the little boy recovered. Three years later, however, the McCullochs did not receive the same miracle when the boy, now six years old, died after being unwell for several months. Even then, he was a fighter, with his obituary stating, "The little fellow's life was despaired of some weeks since, but tenaciously he continued the struggle."[123]

Losing a child at any age is painful, even if they did make it to adulthood. Sarah Ross lost her twenty-eight-year-old daughter Julia to tuberculosis in 1905. The body was prepared by the El Paso undertakers Nagley & Carr, Minnie Nagley's establishment, which also employed Josefa Estrada. Dewey Finnegan, the daughter of lady undertaker Florence Waters, died in 1925, aged twenty-five. Her obituary noted that Finnegan had been "an invalid all her life but her condition did not become critical until a short time before her death, which came as a great shock to her family and friends."[124]

Joseph Ryan, twenty-three-year-old son of Alma Ryan, died from injuries sustained in a car accident in 1928. He'd come home from the University of Texas–Austin to visit his family and went to a St. Patrick's Day dance. Driving home at 4:00 a.m., he flipped the car on a sharp curve and suffered a crushed skull. He died a few hours later.

In 1921, Rosie Cheverere not only lost her daughter but was also put through a roller coaster legal saga after her loss. Hazel Cheverere was twenty-two when she died of "poisoning by bichloride of mercury," according to

The Boerne Reading Club, 1929. The inscription on the back of the photo indicates that Ella Ebensberger is in the middle of the back row, looking to her left. *Patrick Heath Public Library.*

her death certificate. The Science History Institute explains that this was not an uncommon way to die in the period, as mercury bichloride, while very dangerous, was prescribed for various maladies, including syphilis.[125]

A few months later, a man named Robert Jones was arrested and charged with Hazel's murder. He was eventually convicted and sentenced to twenty years for the killing, but he served just six months after the Court of Criminal Appeals found that not only was there no evidence that he'd committed the crime, if anything the evidence pointed the other way, as he was very fond of the young woman. Reading between the lines of various newspaper reports from the case, it seems most likely that Hazel and the married Jones were having an affair and that she died by suicide, leaving a note that mentioned her lover's name.

MURDER

While only one woman undertaker from the period—Lucile Gunter, who shot her husband—appears to have committed murder herself, two others found themselves embroiled in murder trials.

Before moving just across the border to Beaumont, Rena Hebert lived in Louisiana. There, in 1927, she was questioned as a key witness to a murder. A doctor was having an affair with a married woman, and the two enlisted the help of third man to kill the woman's husband. The husband was shot while boating with the other three, according to police, and his body was cut up. The conspirators were arrested, and Hebert was able to vouch for the affair between the doctor and the woman, as Hebert was their go-between, delivering letters between the two.

Carl Stewart worked as an undertaker alongside his mother, Alice Stewart, in Corsicana. Then, in 1932, he was charged with murder. The state alleged that Carl had lured a wealthy and successful Austin undertaker from his funeral parlor and then kidnapped him. Once Carl had the victim in his car, he drove a long distance, beat the man with rocks and then shot him. While the motive was unclear, police thought there was a financial angle to the crime. Alice Stewart was charged as an accessory after the fact, as she had gone to pick up her son after the murder and drove him back to Corsicana. Carl Stewart was sentenced to death and was executed in the electric chair at Huntsville Prison on December 29, 1933.

Widowhood

Many women undertakers worked alongside their husbands, shouldering the burdens of the heavy emotions and nontraditional hours of the demanding industry. When they became widows, they lost not only their life partner but also their business partner, making the loss that much more painful.

Minnie Nagley's husband died after a long battle with tuberculosis in 1910, a far-too-common cause of death in the period. When Ella Fall's husband, John, fell ill and died in 1912, she refused to keep up appearances. She was broken by the loss and would not pretend otherwise. A notice in the *Waco Morning News* eleven days after he died explained, "Many friends have sought to relieve the grief of Mrs. John Fall. She has had every assurance of sympathy, and is bearing greatly under her great sorrow. However, she is still unable to assume the old order of her life yet a while."[126] (Fellow lady undertaker Viola Shelley attended John Fall's funeral.)

By 1930, Dora Dobbins and her husband, Clyde, had fled the scandal caused by accusations of burying a child in a disgraceful manner and moved their undertaking establishment to New Mexico. He owned at least one building that he leased as an investment, as during an argument with the tenant over rent, Dobbins was shot multiple times. Dora witnessed the shooting. Clyde died on the way to the hospital, and the gunman was charged with murder.

Willie Rix's husband, Ralph, did not die with his boots on, as it were. He was asleep in bed with Willie when he suddenly sat up, called her name and

AVISO

Debido a la reciente muerte de Sr. Shelley, anunciamos al público que la AGENCIA DE INHUMACIONES SHELLEY, establecida en San Antonio desde hace más de 30 años, continuará girando sus negocios en el mismo local, esquina de Main Avenue y Travis St.,

Bajo la inspección personal de

MRS. JOE SHELLEY

San Antonio was a particularly cosmopolitan city in this period, with newspapers in English, Spanish and German. This 1922 announcement by Viola Shelley was an exact translation of one that also appeared in English. *From* La Prensa.

died of a heart attack in 1936. As he was only thirty-one years old, this was unexpected, although it was reported that he'd been diagnosed with a heart issue a few years before.

One of the unique problems faced by women who were in business with their husbands was the assumption that their funeral homes would close after the man in their life died. This appears to have been a pattern across many decades, as there were multiple women who felt the need to put notices in the paper that they were continuing their business despite becoming widows. There is an edge to Kate Lowe stating in 1900 that "contrary to circulated reports" she was still working as an undertaker. The same was true in 1924, when Leila Goldman "[denied] persistent rumors" with "absolutely no foundation" that she has gone out of business.

While Viola Shelley made a similar announcement in 1922 (in both English- and Spanish-language newspapers in San Antonio), as did Isabel Sutherland in 1928, it does not sound like they were doing it to head off local gossip that they were closing up shop. (While Sutherland did end up selling her funeral home only months later, she stayed on as vice-president of the company and was involved with it until her death.)

Retirement

Eventually, most lady undertakers decided to hang up their embalming kits and enjoy retirement. Despite their shared vocation, they dedicated themselves to very different passions in their golden years. Many stayed near their families, helping to raise grandchildren.

Others concentrated on existing hobbies. Maggie Bills and her husband, Clarence, retired from the funeral business relatively early and dedicated themselves to raising horses. They eventually turned this into a second career, owning a business that bred and trained the animals, and the couple's own horses won awards in various competitions. Meanwhile, Grace Peak and her brother became serious big game hunters, taking months-long trips to Africa and Asia to shoot things even when still working in the undertaking business; after they retired, they dedicated themselves almost completely to blood sport, even donating a taxidermized lion to a museum.

While some women undertakers saw themselves become young widows, others entered old age with their husbands, like Trudy and Cecil Dennis, who celebrated their fiftieth wedding anniversary in 1975.

Retirement was not for everyone. Whether they loved the work too much to stop or just didn't want to be bored or any number of other possible reasons, some lady undertakers were on the job until they themselves were one foot in the grave. Then in her mid-eighties, Sarah Kinney was still working and training morticians in 1981, just months before she died. Jessie Freund received multiple honors for spending fifty years in the business, including on the fiftieth anniversary of opening her own parlor in 1974. She finally retired in 1985 but was honored for her many decades in the profession by the Texas Funeral Directors Association in 1987, the year before she died.

A LADY UNDERTAKER DIES

Are undertakers more prepared to face death than the average person? Eventually, sometimes too soon, the early lady undertakers of Texas went to their graves. Their deaths were as varied as those of the bodies they had prepared over the years.

Jesse Bower was only twenty-seven years old when she died in 1904 after a weeks-long illness. Annie Ludwig underwent a major, if unspecified, operation in 1912. While she survived the initial surgery, something evidently went wrong, and she died six weeks later.

Some couples can't bear to be apart, even when separated by death. Emily Sneddon and her husband had been married for forty-three years when he passed away in 1917. Emily did not long outlive him, dying just two weeks later.

Josefa Estrada's death was particularly dramatic. After a fight with the youngest of her four daughters, Rachel, the young woman left her home in

El Paso for three days to stay at a hotel. While Josefa knew where Rachel was and sent many friends, family members and even a police officer to convince her daughter to come home, Rachel refused. Finally, Josefa went to see Rachel herself. The mother and daughter were having a heated conversation on the street in front of the hotel when Josefa collapsed and died of a heart attack. Rachel was distraught, and her sisters said that she blamed herself for her mother's death.

LAYING THE LADY UNDERTAKER TO REST

The families of some lady undertakers chose to have the competition prepare the deceased's body and conduct the funeral, for understandable reasons. But other lady undertakers, or their loved ones, chose to be in death the same place they were so often in life, their own establishment.

After Josefa Estrada's sudden death at sixty in 1930, the *El Paso Evening Post* reported that her body "lay dead in a simple gray casket in the little front room of the place where she conducted hundreds of funerals." Lottie Johnston's body lay in state at her own funeral home in 1946, although a different mortuary was in charge of the arrangements.

Irma Griggs not only selected her own funeral home for her laying-in-state when she died in 1965 but also specified that her coffin remain closed during her funeral, an educated decision one can assume she made after attending and performing thousands of funerals over the years.

The graves of the lady undertakers vary from simple, flat slabs to large family mausoleums and everything in between. Most elected for simple inscriptions of their name and dates, sometimes with a tasteful carved flower or cross or the epitaph "Mother."

Anna E. Beck's gravestone is a work of art, a large slab or rough-hewn rock with a carved vine emerging from the bottom front corner, as if it was returning to nature after hundreds of years. Susie Hewett's wide double headstone that she shares with her husband, Arthur, is one of the simplest kinds, except that the names of her and Arthur are carved in the design of their own distinct signatures. Annie and Albert Ludwig share a white Spanish-style mausoleum, with two faux logs carved from stone inset in alcoves on the front, indicating their association with the fraternal order Woodmen of the World. Thelma Hurley and her husband Millard's joint tombstone includes an extra date inscribed on it: December 27, 1921, the day they were married. Many Black women undertakers, including Katie Lee Childs and Narcissa Horton, are buried in what were then the "colored" sections of the cemeteries.

In the saddest turn of events for these women who dedicated part or all of their lives to laying to rest others with dignity, some no longer have any grave markers at all, if they ever did.

Epilogue

1930

Undertaking in Texas, 1930

Undertakers are no more. They have become funeral directors.
Such was the decision of the Texas Funeral Directors and Embalmers
association, in annual meeting [in Dallas] *today.*[127]
—"If 'Undertaker' Is Passe, Whyn't Say 'Mortician,'"
Waxahachie Daily Light, *May 21, 1930*

At its 1930 convention, the state body made it official, changing the name of the organization from the Texas Undertakers and Embalmers Association. While the names had been used somewhat interchangeably for years, especially by reporters, this proved the group was only moving forward, not looking back.

Edgar H. Fatheree of the Kerrville Funeral Parlor flew to that year's convention in Dallas from San Antonio, something so modern and novel that it merited mention in the newspaper (only six thousand people in the whole country flew in a commercial plane that year).[128]

One man who grew up in Victoria around this time remembered how Kate Lowe's establishment was out of business and boarded up, but the trappings of the funeral home had not been removed. He and other boys snuck in the building to box among the coffins: "About 104 E. Commercial St. the old closed-up A. Lowe Undertaking sheds and horse drawn hearse house were located. The doors could be pulled open enough for boys to slip inside. Here among the old hearse and other stores funeral equipment some mighty first cuffs took place. Mostly daring and double dog daring, but it was fun to watch."[129]

Zerva Tapp's establishment, on the other hand, placed a "special announcement for 1930" in the newspaper, explaining how it was "keeping up with the march of progress" in the funeral industry at the dawn of this new decade.

Malloy & Son, the funeral home both Evelyn Malloy and Rosie Cheverere worked for, also saw 1930 as a year to push forward into the future in a big way. The business broke ground on a new building, one that the *Galveston Daily News* called "a far cry from the gloomy, drab 'undertaking parlors' of former days."[130]

Mrs. Floyd Daniels attended the annual convention with her husband,[131] where Annie Belle Eberely of Big Spring was elected third vice-president of the association.[132]

In perhaps the clearest sign, even more than the association changing its name, there was another event in 1930 that proved that the early era of

The inscription on the back of this photo reads, "Mrs. Yokley entertaining the 'Aid,'" circa 1910. Anna Mary Beetham is the formidable-looking woman standing second from the left in the back row. *Boyce Ditto Public Library.*

Texas undertakers was truly at an end. On December 28, 1930, Anna Mary Beetham died in Mineral Wells at the age of seventy-six. She had been in failing health for two years and quickly nearing the end for two weeks.

Mrs. Beetham was buried at Mineral Wells' Elmwood Cemetery, joining her husband who was laid to rest there twenty years before. Their graves have since been lost.

One year after his mother's death, Robert Beetham ran an ad in the *Mineral Wells Index*. It read:

> *A Good Way to Judge a funeral director is by the number of years he has been practicing his profession. Only years of actual, practical experience can teach a funeral director all the finer points of his profession, and equip him to render the type of service that can be rendered by a thoroughly equipped and long experience member of the profession. In the light of these facts, it is interesting to note that the Beetham organization was established in 1882.*[133]

Anna Mary Beetham, the founder of the business, was not mentioned. The world had moved on.

Appendix

LIST OF WOMEN UNDERTAKERS
OF TEXAS, 1880–1930

W hat follows is an incomplete list of women who were employed as undertakers, embalmers or funeral directors at any point between 1880 and 1930. Due to the limitations of sources like Ancesty and Newspapers.com, as well as the availability—or not—of documents at various Texas organizations and universities (not to mention the limitations of the researcher), there is no way to make a complete record of these groundbreaking women.

The loss of the majority of the 1890 census records in a fire in 1921, and the U.S. government's purposeful destruction of virtually all of the remaining records in 1934–35, was a disastrous blow to projects like this one. However, every effort has been made to identify women who worked as undertakers during this period.

With only a few exceptions, this list is limited to women who were specifically described as embalmers, undertakers, funeral directors or morticians on at least one historical document. There are just as many women who worked for funeral homes in positions such as bookkeepers, stenographers, office managers, organists and all the other jobs that keep such businesses running, but they are not included on this list.

In general, the information about the women listed here is limited to their connection to the funeral business, rather than events in their personal lives. They are listed alphabetically by the last name they most commonly used in their career, regardless of if they later married and changed their name.

ADAMS, MAMIE B. *NORCROSS* (January 15, 1887–June 26, 1981): Recorded as an "undertaker in town" on the 1920 census in Joshua, Johnson County.

ANDREWS, ELMA H. (November 2, 1904 or 1905–October 3, 1987): Recorded as an embalmer on the 1930 and 1950 censuses in Lufkin, Angelina County and Houston, respectively.

BAUMGARTEN, OTTILIE *WOLTERS* (May 22, 1876–June 10, 1971): Recorded as an undertaker in the 1910 census, with the Baumgarten-Schwenke, Embalmers, in Schulenburg, Fayette County. One of the fifteen Texas women undertakers profiled in the 1912 syndicated newspaper article.

BECK, ANNA ELIZABETH *HEINSEN* (1863–May 22, 1920): Recorded as an embalmer in the 1920 census, with Beck Mortuary in Yoakum, DeWitt County. First wife of the proprietor, Andrew E. Beck, who went on to marry Elma Beck after Anna's death. One of the fifteen Texas women undertakers profiled in the 1912 syndicated newspaper article.

BECK, ELMA "SIM" *BEAL* MACK (March 15, 1888–December 22, 1980): Recorded as a funeral director on the 1940 census and as a mortician on her death certificate, with Beck Mortuary in Yoakum, DeWitt County, followed by Beck-Geiger Funeral Home in Hallettsville, Lavaca County. Second wife of the proprietor, Andrew E. Beck, after the death of his first wife, Anna Beck. The subject of the semi-biographical one-woman play *SIM: One Night with a Lady Undertaker from Texas*, written by William Osborn.

BEENE, HATTIE L. *MIMMS* (February 10, 1896–February 6, 1978): Her attendance at the 1928 Texas State Undertakers Convention in Mineral Wells was reported in the May 17 edition of the *Corsicana Daily Sun*. Husband Jesse Minor Beene was recorded as an undertaker in the 1930 census, with the Beene Brothers Furniture and Undertaking Company in Frost, Navarro County.

BEETHAM, ANNA MARY *ANTHES* (September 22, 1854–December 28, 1930): Founder of A.M. Beetham, Undertaker—later Beetham & Son—in Mineral Wells, Palo Pinto and Parker Counties in 1882.

BERRIEN, ELIZA L. *GUGERTY* (May 30, 1860–August 5, 1919): In 1903, the *El Paso Herald* reported that Eliza planned to take the embalmer exam the following month, which would mean all four members of the Emerson & Berrien undertaking company—including Willie Horner—would be licensed embalmers.

BILLS, MAGGIE ALICE *FARMER* (February 18, 1896–October 20, 1967): Recorded as an embalmer in the 1920 census and as a mortician on her death certificate, in Hillsboro, Hills County.

BLESSING, HATTIE MAE *ELLIS* (1888–January 10, 1968): Assisted her husband at the T.E. Blessing Funeral Home in Mansfield, Tarrant County, after their marriage circa 1910. Received her embalming license in 1935.

BOWER, JESSE M. (August 9, 1877–August 4, 1904): Recorded as an undertaker and resident of Jefferson, Marion County, in the 1900 census.

BOXWELL, IRENE A. *GEISER* (December 30, 1903–March 13, 1995): Advertised as the "lady attendant," assistant and soloist at Boxwell Brothers Funeral Home of Amarillo, Randall County, beginning in 1929. Was still employed with the company as of 1958.

BRANCH, LENA H. (?–?): Advertised as a lady attendant with Navarro Mortuary in Corsicana, Navarro County, in 1922. Also the secretary of the Colored Mutual Protection Association of Corsicana, which paid out $500 on the death of a policy holder.

BRICKEL, CLARA ALICE *NEWLAND* (March 26, 1865–June 11, 1960): The *Houston Post* reported she was attending the 1916 Texas Undertakers Convention with her husband, James Wesley Brickel, and their daughter, the future Leila Goldman.

BROWN, MILLIE (circa 1887–?): Married to S.M. Brown, who in 1916 was manager of the Fraternal Undertaking Company, "the only colored undertaking establishment in Gainesville." Sometime after Lucile Gunter shot and killed her husband in 1919, the Browns took over the Citizens Mortuary in Dallas. In 1921, the business advertised Millie as a licensed embalmer who made "a specialty of lady subjects."

BRULIN HOTCHKISS, LORENA *WUNDERLE* (August 26, 1893–February 5, 1952): Recorded as a "lady embalmer" in the 1930 census and as a funeral

An ambulance of the Pipkin & Brulin Company was put into service as a hearse during the 1926 mass funeral in Port Arthur for the twenty-five men who burned to death in the explosion of the oil tanker *Gulf of Venezuela*. Two further men were reported missing, and at least one other seaman would die from his wounds after the initial disaster. *Museum of the Gulf Coast.*

director on her death certificate. During the 1920s, the Beaumont, Jefferson County directory lists her as the "Assistant in Care Ladies and Children" at Pipkin & Brulin Company. Elected second vice-president of the Texas Funeral Directors Association in 1927.

BUFFINGTON FRY, RUBY *Ross* (July 11, 1885–March 18, 1970): Recorded in the 1920 census as an assistant manager with the Buffington Undertaking Company, later renamed Buffington Funeral Home, in Yoakum, Lavaca County. She sold the business to Byron Dixon in 1947 after the death of her husband, Ludlow Dwight Buffington.

BURNETT, HELLA (POSSIBLY "DELLA") (November 1871–?): Recorded as an undertaker in San Antonio, Bexar County, in the 1900 census. It is possible she was associated with J.T. Burnett & Company.

BYNUM, VERA *PILLEY* (October 30, 1900–April 17, 1993): A registered nurse; according to her obituary, after 1926 she joined her husband, Luther H. Bynum, in the Bynum Bros. undertaking firm in Lubbock. She was recorded as an embalmer in the 1930 census.

CARTER, ANNIE EDITH (circa 1872–July 3, 1964): Proprietor of the Carter Sutton Funeral Directors (later renamed the Carter Undertaking Company and subsequently the Carter-Taylor Mortuary) in San Antonio, Bexar County, after the death of her husband in 1927. Purchased Eastview Cemetery in 1942 and renamed it Southern Memorial Parks Inc. Recorded as a funeral director on her death certificate.

CHEVERERE, ROSE "ROSIE" *MILLER* (December 28, 1887–April 5, 1948): Married Joseph R. Cheverere circa 1901; by 1909 he was working as an embalmer for Evelyn Malloy's future father-in-law in Galveston. In 1913, Joseph was the funeral director and licensed embalmer at the city's Prater Undertaking Company, which advertised a "lady assistant" and "lady attendant when desired," most likely his wife, Rosie.

CHILDS LEWIS, KATIE *LEE* (December 13, 1888–January 4, 1938): The May 21, 1917 edition of the *Sherman Daily Democrat* reported she had passed her embalming exams and would assist her husband, Daniel, at the Childs Undertaking Company, both "the oldest undertaker establishment for colored people" and owner of the "only colored hearse in Sherman," Grayson County. Katie was recorded as the manager of an undertaking business in the 1920 census. The November 6, 1920 edition of the *Dallas Express* reported she was the assistant secretary of the Texas State Embalmers Association.

CLARK, M.A. (?–?): The only woman of color mentioned in the 1912 syndicated newspaper article profiling fifteen Texas women undertakers. However, other than including her (partial) name on the list of women within the article and the fact that she lived in Clarksville, Red River County, M.A. Clark is never mentioned again in the piece. Despite much searching, I have been unable to find any further information on her.

DANIEL, LUCILLE IVA *MCALLISTER* (November 23, 1888–October 23, 1974): Married Floyd Daniel circa 1912; as of the 1920 census he was working as an undertaker. Lucille attended the 1930 convention of the Texas Funeral

Directors and Embalmers Association and by 1933 was advertised as a "lady assistant" with the Burke-Walker Funeral Home in Tyler, Smith County, where her husband was vice-president.

DANNEL, FLOSSIE LOUELLA *WADE* (January 6, 1888–October 1, 1981): Shortly after her marriage to John C. Dannel circa 1908, the couple moved from Illinois to Sherman, Grayson County. They purchased the Sherman Undertaking Company, renaming it the John C. Dannel Undertaking Company, although both the current Dannel Funeral Home website and Texas Historical Commission Marker and an analysis of the business's early funeral records[134] indicate that Flossie was her husband's partner in the business.

DAVENPORT, REBECCA "BECKY" (June 1859–April 1925): Recorded as an undertaker in the 1900 census, living in Calvert, Robertson County.

DAVIS, LILLIAN N. (circa 1894–?): Recorded as an assistant embalmer in an undertaking establishment in the 1920 census for Houston, Harris County. A wage worker, by 1930 she was employed in a shoe store.

DAWSON, IDA *HYDER* (circa 1885–?): Recorded as an embalmer at the undertaking company owned by her husband, James Joseph "J.J." Dawson, in Temple, Bell County, on the 1920 census. By 1921, she had moved to Oklahoma City, where J.J. Dawson & Company advertised its "unique service" of a "lady attendant."

DENNING, ELIZABETH ANNE *DENMARK* (December 6, 1878–April 29, 1925): In 1912, she moved to San Angelo, Tom Green County, with her husband, W. Jack Denning, to run the funeral department of the Angelo Furniture & Undertaking Company. Advertised as a "competent lady assistant." Sister-in-law of Fannie Denning.

DENNING, FANNIE *HEFFNER* (May 2, 1885–January 1, 1958): Married to David Denning of the Denning & Ragsdale undertaking establishment in Marlin, Falls County. In 1924, she attended the convention of the National Undertakers association with her husband, and the following year, the *Waco News-Tribune* reported she was returning to the national convention as a delegate. Sister-in-law of Elizabeth Denning.

DENNIS, TRUDY *BROWN* (March 9, 1905–November 25, 1985): A trained nurse, she entered the funeral business when she married Landrum Cecil Dennis in 1925. In 1928, they opened the Dennis Funeral Parlor in Cooper, Delta County, with Trudy an equal partner along with her husband and father-in-law. By 1929, she had earned her embalmers license, and the company advertised a "lady embalmer on all calls." As late as 1932, ads claimed she was the "only lady embalmer in Delta County." Her obituary notes that she was a licensed funeral director for more than thirty years.

DEQUOY, IDA AMELIA (November 13, 1875–December 9, 1954): Recorded as an embalmer at an undertaking parlor in the 1920 and 1930 censuses, as well as the 1930 Galveston City Directory. In its June 2, 1914 edition, the *Galveston Tribune* reported that she had passed her exams and received her embalmers license; she was employed by F.P. Malloy & Son in that city. However, she incorrectly believed that she was "the only woman undertaker in the state of Texas." Her license from the Texas State Board of Embalming, dated May 29, 1914, is held by the Galveston & Texas History Center.

DOBBINS, DORA BELLE *MOLLETT* (December 1876–August 13, 1958): Advertised as a "lady attendant" or "lady assistant" with the Dobbins & Son Funeral Home in Borger, Hutchinson County, during 1927.

DURST, FANNIE *DEARMON* (April 15, 1889–January 8, 1946): Recorded as an "Undertaker Helper" in the 1920 census. Port Arthur city directories listed her changing job description over the decades as a clerk with Smith, Moody & Company in 1929; an attendant with the T.J. Miles Undertaking Company in 1931; and an employee (1933), clerk (1936), maid (1938), attendant (1941) and helper (1945) with (L.M.) Moody's Funeral Home. While it is unclear based on this information if she was involved in preparing bodies or arranging funerals, the fact that she worked in the funeral industry for at least twenty-five years, and as a Black woman may not have been given a title that reflected her responsibilities, it is reasonable to assume that as a "helper" and "attendant" she was more involved in the business than the titles of "maid" or "clerk" would convey.

EAST, QUEEN E. "QUEENIE" *VAUGHN* (1870–1932): Founded the East Undertaking Company in Texarkana in 1898 with her husband, Elias C. "E.C." East. The modern East Funeral Home's website notes, "A female attendant was always in waiting for the care of women and children....After

E.C. died in 1908, his widow…continued in the business with the same policies." Queen is recorded as the "proprietress" of an undertaking parlor in the 1910 census. While she sold the business in 1911, she remained involved in its running, with the 1917 Texarkana City Directory listing her as the secretary and treasurer of the East Undertaking Company, and the 1930 census recorded that she worked as an assistant at an undertaking parlor. (Strangely, the 1920 census recorded she was employed as a forewoman at a casket company.)

EBENSBERGER, ELLA *AMMANN* (August 20, 1887–March 10, 1976): Her husband, Edmund "Ed" Walter Ebensberger, took over his father's businesses in Boerne, Kendall County, including an undertaking and lumber concern, in 1907. Two years later, Ella married Ed, and she would go on to get her funeral director's license, according to the Ebensberger-Fisher Funeral Home website.

EBERLEY, ANNIE BELLE *GREEN* (November 18, 1898–April 19, 1970): Opened the Eberley Funeral Home in Big Spring, Howard County, with her husband, Charles, in 1920. She was listed as the business's manager in the 1928 Big Spring City Directory, while in 1930 her role was advertised as "lady assistant"; in the 1930 census, she was recorded as a "laborer" at her husband's undertaking establishment. That same year, she was elected vice-president of the Texas Funeral Directors and Embalmers Association; in 1947, she was secretary-treasurer of the Central West Texas Funeral Directors and Embalmers Association. Recorded as a retired funeral director on her death certificate.

ELLIS MOORE, GERTRUDE (October 16. 1890–June 27, 1973): As Miss Gertrude Ellis of Toyah, Reeves County, she was one of the fifteen Texas women undertakers profiled in the 1912 syndicated newspaper article. However, by the time the article ran, she was married to Francis L. Moore of El Paso.

ESTRADA, JOSEFA *BERMUDEZ* VDA. DE (January 29, 1870–September 7, 1930): While the census did not list an occupation (undertaker) for her until 1930, after her husband's death in 1911, subsequent El Paso city directories note that she was the proprietor of Pedro Estrada & Company, as did the New Mexico State Business Directory in 1921. She was recorded as an undertaker on her death certificate, and her obituary in the September 9, 1930 edition of the *El Paso Times* reported she had "for many years conducted undertaking parlors" in the city.

EWING, ANNIE J. (circa 1885–?): Recorded as an undertaker on the 1930 census and associated with the People's Undertaking Company of Dallas. Her husband, William E. Ewing, was president of the firm.

FAIRCHILD, MARY E. "MAMIE" *HOWARD* (Jul 17, 1880–December 12, 1961): Recorded as a bookkeeper in the 1920 census and a secretary in the 1930 census, both at the Fairchild Undertaking Company of Houston, Harris County, which was run by her husband, Thornton McNair Fairchild.

FALL SMITH, ELLA *WEMPLE* (April 1, 1871–January 5, 1941): One of the fifteen Texas women undertakers profiled in the 1912 syndicated newspaper article. After her husband, John Gilbert Fall, died on January 9, 1912, the Fall & Puckett Undertaking business of Waco, McLennan County, dissolved, and she opened the John Fall Undertaking Company with her son. In April 1912, Ella was elected second vice-president of the Texas Funeral Directors and Embalmers' Association. That same month, the *Fort Worth Star-Telegram* reported (incorrectly) that she was one of only two women undertakers in Texas. The 1913 Waco City Directory listed her as the proprietor of the business; however, by then it was no longer in existence, having closed on November 13, 1912.

FEATHER, SUSAN *BROWN* (April 27, 1868–September 15, 1957): Her husband, Merton Kerr Feather, announced the opening of his undertaking company in Palacios, Matagorda County, in November 1919, promising a "lady attendant for women's and children's cases when desired."

FINDLEY, THEODOSIA "DOSIA" *LEARN* (April 2, 1889–July 23, 1980): After the death of her husband, Walter Abe Findley, in 1926 (his funeral was directed by Alma Ryan's husband, Joseph), Dosia took sole control of their undertaking establishment in Edna, Jackson County, and was recorded as the owner on the 1930 census.

FLEMING, ARIZONA (March 23, 1884 or 1898–January 18, 1976): An icon of the civil rights movement, she co-founded a funeral home in Richmond to serve the Black residents of Fort Bend County in 1927. Within a few years she was the sole proprietor. The 1930 and 1950 censuses record that she was an undertaker and funeral director, respectively. The Arizona Fleming Elementary School of the Fort Bend Independent School District is named after her.

FOGLE, JEANETTE *WILCOX* (August 20, 1891–October 4, 1975): Married to Ray Fogle, manager of the Fogle-West Undertaking Company in Houston. The business advertised a lady attendant from at least 1920, including in 1924: "We have at all times in our Undertaking Department a lady attendant to render aid to children and ladies who should have special care."[135]

FOUST, DAISY ADAIR *HUITT* (September 5, 1876–March 31, 1963): Texas Historical Commission marker 8673 records, "John E. Foust (1861–1926) moved to Grapevine in 1880 and started a general merchandise store which stocked coffins. He gradually added other services and with the help of his wife Daisy (Huitt) (1876–1963) established a funeral company." The business advertised a lady assistant.

FOX, ROBBIE INEZ *FANNING* (February 5, 1905–June 29, 1983): Recorded as an embalmer on the 1930 and 1940 census and the director of a funeral home on the 1950 census, in Van Alstyne, Grayson County.

FREUND, JOSIE B. *MUELLER* (July 21, 1895–March 29, 1988): Her obituary notes that she first started in undertaking business in 1924 and that she and her husband, E.J. Freund, built their own establishment, the Freund Funeral Home in Cuero, DeWitt County, in 1928. The 1930 census records that she was the bookkeeper for the business, and in 1937, she announced in the *Cuero Record* that she had "assumed full control" of the funeral home. She sold the company in 1946; however, she continued to work there until 1985, and the 1950 census records that she was employed as a funeral director. In 1987, the Texas Funeral Directors Association recognized her fifty years of service in the funeral industry.

FULLER, VIOLET (circa 1906–?): Fuller, then twenty-four, roomed in the same boardinghouse as Dorothy Hogle in Fort Worth in 1930. The census records Fuller was a student at an otherwise anonymous "Undertaking Co."

GASSAWAY STUART, RUIE ELLA *HUDSON* THORNTON (December 29, 1899–February 20, 1984): Recorded as an assistant embalmer in Greenville, Hunt County, in the 1930 census.

GEHRIG, CORAL VAIN *JONES* (circa 1880–March 22, 1956): Recorded as an embalmer in Dallas on the 1930 census. While the business was not named, it is likely it was Sparkman-Holtz-Brand, which various Dallas city directories of the 1940s list her as working for.

GOLDMAN WANGEMAN, LEILA *BRICKEL* (October 23, 1893–August 25, 1983): In 1916, before her marriage, the *Houston Post* reported that she was attending the Texas Undertakers convention with her father and mother. The F.L. Goldman undertaking establishment, run by her husband, advertised a lady attendant in 1917. Two years later, after becoming a widow, Leila announced that she would take over the running of the company. In 1920, she was recorded in the census as an embalmer and advertised herself as either the manager or the proprietress until 1928, when she sold the company to the husband of Florence Waters.

The Late
F. L. GOLDMAN'S
UNDERTAKING
ESTABLISHMENT
Is being conducted under the name
of
MRS. F. L. GOLDMAN
With V. E. Goldman as manager
and Mr. Halbert Fall as expert embalmer and funeral director. Lady
attendant. Motor and horse
drawn equipment. Phones, day or
night, 750 or 751.

Leila Goldman was one of several widows who needed to announce that they would be continuing the funeral home they founded with their husbands, although not many of them changed the name of the business to their own, as Goldman did in 1919. *From the* Daily Advocate.

GOODSON, VIOLA MARTHA *MERRITT* (July 2, 1898–March 28, 1973): Viola and her husband, Ray Charles Goodson, opened their first funeral home in Wellington, Collingsworth County, in 1924, which they ran until 1936. The couple opened further funeral homes in Freer, Duval County, as well as three locations in Oklahoma. Viola ended her career as a traveling saleswoman for a funeral supply company. She is recorded as an embalmer on the 1930 and 1940 censuses, in Wellington and Freer, respectively. Her daughter Charlene's wedding announcement in 1948 revealed that Charlene had followed her parents into the business, graduating from the St. Louis College of Mortuary Science.

GRANT MARTIN, ELLA M. (circa 1912–?): Recorded as a student undertaker in Galveston in the 1930 census.

GRIGGS, IRMA HORTENSE *CASSIDY* (October 9, 1900–November 8, 1965): Graduated from the Dallas College of Embalming in 1923, three years after her marriage to J. Horace Griggs of the N.S. Griggs undertaking establishment in Amarillo. Advertised as "specializing in the care of ladies and children" and "the only graduate and licensed lady embalmer in the Panhandle" in the 1920s. Listed as an embalmer in the Amarillo city directories throughout the second half of the 1920s. Recorded as an embalmer on the 1940 census. In a 1961 newspaper profile and her 1965 obituary, it was claimed that she was still the only woman funeral director in Amarillo and "the oldest active woman embalmer in the state."[136]

GUEST, ADLANTA (July 2, 1888–February 1969): Listed as an embalmer with the Neighbor Aid Undertakers in the Paris, Lamar County city directories from at least 1919. Recorded as an embalmer in the 1920 census and a receptionist at her husband George Guest's undertaking company in 1940. In 1923, the *Houston Informer* reported that she was one of the undertakers attending the seventh annual lecture series from the Colored Funeral Directors and Embalmers' Association. After she became a widow in 1948, she closed the business, had the building torn down and donated the land for a nursery school for Black children.

GUNTER, LUCILE (circa 1891–?): Married the undertaker J.P. Gunter of Dallas in 1913; they opened the Citizens Mortuary in June 1918. In November 1919, Lucile shot her husband during an altercation, and he died from his wounds later that day. However, she was released on bail and was still recorded as an undertaker with her own establishment on the 1920 census. By 1921, the Citizens Mortuary was under the management of Millie Brown and her husband.

HAGEDON, ESTHER LOUISE *FRASER* (May 29, 1885–March 16, 1940): Gifted a box of candy from the Toothpick Club—the "fun organization"[137] of the Texas Funeral Directors Association—at the annual convention in 1927, the same year her husband stepped down as president of the club. In 1924, the Peak-Hagedon Funeral Home of El Paso advertised "lady attendants—trained and thoughtful—always in attendance." The other lady attendant at the business was probably Grace Peak, sister and companion of J.W. Peak.

The "trained and thoughtful" women at Peak-Hagedon mentioned in this 1924 ad were Esther Hagedon, wife of Barry Hagedon, and Grace Peak, sister of J.W. Peak. *From the* El Paso Times.

HARGROVE, BALLA *HARRIS* (October 5, 1861–October 25, 1934): The local paper reported that she'd returned to Marshall, Harrison County, to attend the undertakers' convention in 1923.

HATCHELL, ADA (March 19, 1879–January 6, 1971): Assisted her father, Amster Allen Hatchell, in his undertaking business until his death in 1939. Recorded as an assistant embalmer in Crosbyton, Crosby County, on the 1930 census.

HEBERT, RENA *BOWENS* CLICK (September 22, 1885–July 10, 1939): The 1930 census records that she "helps in undertaking shop," the Peoples Undertaking Company in Beaumont, Jefferson County.

HENDERSON, BESS ELLA "BESSIE" *WHITESIDE* (November 22, 1892–January 15, 1974): Most likely the lady assistant advertised with her husband T.A. Henderson's undertaking establishment of Weatherford, Parker County, in 1912.

HENDERSON, MRS. CHARLES (?–?): Advertised as a "competent lady assistant" with the Chas. R. Henderson undertaking establishment of El Paso until June 1901. After Minnie Nagley's husband left the city's competing firm Nagley, Lyons & McBean that month, the Hendersons went to work for the newly named McBean, Lyons & Company.

HEWETT (ALSO SPELLED "HEWITT"), SUSIE E. *MIDKIFF* (December 2, 1876–July 31, 1969): In 1915, the *Fort Worth Star-Telegram* reported that she was one of just three women to receive their embalming license in that year's examinations. Attended the 1917 Texas Funeral Directors Convention in Dallas with her husband, Arthur James Hewett. Recorded as an embalmer and an undertaker on the 1930 and 1950 censuses, respectively, and as a licensed funeral director and mortician on her death certificate.

HICKMAN, EDYTHE *BRYAN* (August 28, 1877–January 2, 1963): In 1920, the *Mercedes Tribune* (Hidalgo County) reported that Edythe and her husband, Ross Hickman, had accepted positions at the H.J. Menton Mercantile Company. The couple had been working together in the funeral industry in Oklahoma and Missouri for three decades. While advertised as a lady assistant, Edythe's obituary says that she was a licensed funeral director into her eighties.

HILLIER, MARGARET *WARD* (September 4, 1893–January 14, 1982): Worked with her husband, Charles F. Hillier, at the McCulloch-Gordon Company, later the McCulloch-Dansby Company, before founding the Hillier Funeral Home in Bryan, Brazos County. Margaret was advertised as a lady attendant. The *Eagle* reported almost yearly on the couple's attendance at the Texas Funeral Directors Convention from at least 1923 to 1949.

HINES, SALLIE FAYNE *SMITH* (August 6, 1884–April 8, 1964): Advertised as the assistant to her husband, Oscar W. Hines, at the Wichita Falls Undertaking Company in 1914. The town's 1921 city directory lists Sallie as an assistant to her husband again, this time in a firm under his own name. The *Wichita Falls Times* reported that the couple attended the Texas State Funeral Directors annual convention in 1927 and 1934. The 1930 census records that Sallie was a bookkeeper at the mortuary.

HOGLE BYLER, DOROTHY (August 10, 1908–January 2, 1983): Hogle, then twenty-two, roomed in the same boardinghouse as Violet Fuller in Fort Worth in 1930. The census records that Hogle was an embalmer at an otherwise anonymous "Undertaking Co."

HORNER, WILLIE BRANDON *MILLS* (circa 1878–January 15, 1920): In 1901, the El Paso Coffin & Casket Company was advertising a lady assistant at its establishment; by the next year, she was a "licensed lady embalmer." However, Willie did not actually take the exams for her license until 1903, to comply with the state's change in law. Her examinations were covered extensively in the press. The *El Paso Herald* included at least half a dozen pieces on her accomplishment, while the *Southern Messenger* (San Antonio) found it notable that she was the only Catholic woman to take the exam. Some of the articles claimed that she was the first woman to qualify as an embalmer under the new law; it is likely that this is true either for her or Bettie Lattner, who also passed the exams that year. The 1903 El Paso City Directory lists Willie as an embalmer with the El Paso Coffin & Casket Company; however, by the time the 1907 version was released, she was with Peak & Horner. The latter company advertised her as "the only licensed lady embalmer in the city." She is recorded as an embalmer on the 1910 census and was one of the fifteen Texas women undertakers profiled in the 1912 syndicated newspaper article.

HORTON, NARCISSA (April 12, 1871–December 4, 1935): Recorded as an undertaker in the "caskets" industry on the 1930 census. Her death certificate lists her professions as "domestic and undertaking business," and the document was signed by the Horton Undertaking Company of Hallettsville, Lavaca County. A short death notice in the town's white newspaper, the *Tribune*, described her as a "colored woman undertaker here for many years."

HURLEY, THELMA ELIZABETH *PIERCE* (September 26, 1903–October 8, 1992): Married Millard C. Hurley, founder of the Hurley Funeral Home in Poteet, Atascosa County, circa 1922. According to the modern funeral home's website, Thelma was heavily involved in the running of the business, down to sewing burial suits and baking cakes for bereaved families.

JACKSON, BLANCHE B. (circa 1887–?): The 1929 and 1932 Houston city directories list her as the manager of the Jackson Undertaking Company. The 1930, 1940 and 1950 censuses record her occupation as undertaker, proprietor of a funeral home and co-owner/president of the funeral home, respectively.

Embalmers Toothpick Club Members Get in Some Practice

Described as "three prominent 'agitators'" of the Toothpick Club, Annie Jennings is pictured with two other members at the undertakers' convention in 1926. For one dollar, which went towards buying gifts for retiring funeral directors, those who joined received a single toothpick. *From the* Fort Worth Star-Telegram.

JENNINGS, ANNIE AGNES *CALCOTE* (October 10, 1894–April 27, 1975): A registered nurse and married to Edwin J. Jennings, a traveling salesman for the National Casket Company for almost five decades. Annie was not an undertaker, but she deserves inclusion as treasurer of the Texas Funeral Directors Association's Toothpick Club from at least 1924 to 1928. In 1925, the club, which celebrated notable and retiring undertakers, gifted Annie a vanity case, and in 1927, she received a box of candy.

JOHNSON, ALMA (March 3, 1887–July 27, 1941): In 1925, Alma was advertised as a lady assistant with the Robinson Undertaking Company of San Angelo, Tom Green County, which was managed by her brother Enoch Johnson. In 1929, the siblings, along with three other partners, opened Johnson's Funeral Home in the same city, where Alma was secretary and treasurer, as well as continued her work as a lady attendant. She was recorded as the proprietor of a funeral home in the 1930 census. She was recorded as a funeral director in the 1940 census, as well as on her death certificate one year later.

JOHNSTON, LOTTIE *GILLETTE* (January 23, 1882–July 25, 1946): According to her obituary, Lottie became a licensed embalmer in 1928 and co-owned the Johnston Funeral Home in Sweetwater, Nolan County, with her husband, Seth. While the 1940 census recorded her as a "helper undertaker," in 1930 she was advertised as an embalmer, equal to her husband. That same year, she attended the Texas Undertakers Association convention, apparently on her own, per reporting in local Sweetwater papers.

JONES, ALTOONA ALLONY "ALICE" *BEAN* (February 16, 1855–June 12, 1932): A widowed single mother recorded as an undertaker in Canton, Van Zandt County, on the 1900 census.

JONES, JOSIE (March 6, 1883–September 12, 1953): Recorded as an embalmer at her husband John Jones's undertaking establishment in Wharton on the 1920 census.

JONES, LIDA E. SAGESER (October 27, 1886–July 7, 1990): In 1930, the Penick-Hughes Company in Stamford, Jones/Haskell Counties, announced that Lida, along with her husband, Virgil E. Jones, who had "several years' experience in the management and operation of funeral homes," would be taking control of the business. Lida would subsequently be advertised as a lady attendant and "in charge of mortuary."

The funeral of W.R. Robison at Abbott Cemetery in Hill County, 1910, illustrates how funerals were events that could bring out the whole community. *Private collection of T.B. Willis.*

KENNARD, CRESSIE L. *RUSSELL* (May 31, 1891–January 13, 1961): Founded the Citizen's Mortuary in Hillsboro, Hill County, with her husband, Willie Clifton Kennard, and Andy Elliott in 1919; the 1920 census records that she was an embalmer in her own parlor. By 1934, the couple owned and operated Kennard Funeral Home in Waco, as listed in the city directory. The 1940 census described Cressie's occupation as "assists husband."

KINNA, MRS. JOHN (?–?): In 1911, the *Austin American-Statesman* reported that undertaker George W. Patterson had introduced a "decided novelty" to the city in the person of Mrs. Kinna, a woman undertaker who had been licensed and working in North Dakota since 1904. Subsequently, she was advertised as a lady assistant.

KINNEY, SARAH LINDA *PURDY* (February 17, 1896–October 5, 1981): A 1981 article in the *Gatesville Messenger and Star-Forum* reported a newly licensed funeral director would be working at the Kinney Funeral Home and continue his training under Sarah Kinney. Originally called the Kinney Furniture and Undertaking Company, it was founded in Stamford, Jones County, in 1929 by John Henry Kinney and his wife, Sarah. Recorded as a mortician's assistant in the 1950 census, as late as the forty-eighth anniversary of the business in 1977, newspapers were reporting that Sarah was the only woman embalmer in the county. Ten months after her mention in the 1981 newspaper article, Sarah's death certificate listed her occupation as funeral director/embalmer.

KREIDLER, HARRIET M. *STEINBACH* (July 29, 1862–April 25, 1946): After operating an undertaking business in Chicago—where, it is claimed, Harriet Kreidler was the first licensed female embalmer in the state—Harriet and Harry Kreidler moved to McAllen, Hidalgo County, and opened the Kreidler Undertaking Company in 1912. She was recorded as an embalmer on the 1920 census, and in a 1932 profile covering the opening of the funeral home's latest location, her role was described as "a wise counsellor through the years in the development of the Kreidler firm."

LATTNER, BETTIE H. *CLEMENTS* (August 16, 1872–March 2, 1945): Possibly the first licensed woman embalmer in Texas. In 1903, she "passed a very credible examination," the first year the text was given.[138] She and her husband opened their furniture and undertaking business in Mineral Wells in or around 1892. Bettie was credited with "capturing" the annual undertaker convention for Mineral Wells in 1904 and was elected the association's second vice-president in 1909. One of the fifteen Texas women undertakers profiled in the 1912 syndicated newspaper article, she retired in 1935.

An undated portrait of Dan T. Laughter, second husband of Lucy Hiatt (née Smith), of the Laughter Undertaking Company in Abilene. *McMurry University Library.*

LAUGHTER, LUCY REBECCA SMITH (September 28, 1883–December 7, 1969): Married Dan T. Laughter Sr., an established undertaker in Abilene, in 1915. According to her obituary in the *Abilene Reporter-News*, for years, the couple "traveled West Texas in a buckboard hitched to a team of horses handling funeral services." She attended the annual undertaker convention often, including in 1929. She and her husband sold the Laughter Funeral Home in 1945.

LEACH, CLARA B. (circa 1897–?): Recorded working as an undertaker in Marshall, Harrison County, in the 1930 census.

LEATHERWOOD, MINNIE IRENE *HOOKS* (February 16, 1882–August 10, 1970): The *Waco News-Tribune* reported that she attended the 1928 Texas Funeral Directors Convention with her husband, R.B. Leatherwood. He was previously president of the association in 1921–22.

LEE, ZENOBIA CARROLL *POPE* (November 16, 1897– July 21, 1977): Founded the Paul U. Lee Funeral Home with her husband in what was then Goose Creek (now Baytown, Harris County) in 1923. She was advertised as a lady assistant, and the 1930 census records Zenobia was an assistant funeral director. The 1940 and 1950 censuses show that she was still actively working at the funeral home, and her obituary states that she only cut back on some of her duties there a few months before she died due to ill health and the insistence of her family. Zenobia died two days after the business's fifty-fourth anniversary. Her death certificate lists her occupation as funeral director.

The future Zenobia Lee pictured in her college yearbook in 1913, from what is now the University of Louisiana–Lafayette. Attakapas was a debate and literary society. *Southwestern Louisiana Industrial Institute.*

LEWIS, GERTRUDE M. (July 17, 1899–November 27, 1985): Married Frank Lewis, an established undertaker in San Antonio, in 1925 and assisted at the Lewis Funeral Home. After Frank's death in 1960, Gertrude continued running the business with her son V.E. Larremore, according to reporting on the seventy-sixth anniversary of the funeral home in 1986.

LIVINGSTON, JO ELLA *FUNK* (April 26, 1902–May 5, 1967): Founded the Livingston Funeral Home in Alpine, Brewster County, with her husband, Charles, in 1924. Her son's 2009 obituary noted (incorrectly) that she was "the second licensed female mortician in Texas." The 1940 census recorded that she was an embalmer and "assist. to husband." She was listed as a mortician on her death certificate.

LOWE, KATHERINE "KATE" OR "KATIE" *SCHULTE* (also spelled *Schoulter* and *Schutter*) (February 25, 1844–January 20, 1926): Married the established undertaker and widower Alexander Lowe of Victoria in 1875. After his death in 1899, she continued his business under her own name, advertising as Mrs. Kate Lowe, and the next year she released a statement in the *Victoria Advocate* that "contrary to circulated reports" the firm was still going strong. She sold the business in 1914.

LUDWIG, ANNIE L. *BRUNS* (April 11, 1865–December 12, 1912): Advertised as the "only lady attendant" by the San Antonio Undertaking and Embalming Company in 1906. (Presumedly this meant she was the only one in the city, although the area was not specified.) Her husband, Albert L. Ludwig, was the proprietor of the business.

MAHON, LENA L. *BISHOP* (circa 1884–?): Assistant and later "lady undertaker" with V.O. Weed in Austin, Travis County. Received her temporary Texas embalming license in September 1904 and her full license in May 1905. One of the fifteen Texas women undertakers profiled in the 1912 syndicated newspaper article.

MALLOY, EVELYN *FACHAN* (circa 1894–August 30, 1985): Joined her husband, Frank R. Malloy Jr., at F.P. Malloy & Son of Galveston after their marriage circa 1911. It was renamed Malloy & Son in 1930, and Evelyn took over as president after the death of her husband in 1957.

MAY-HERRING, MATTIE C. *HOLT* (July 3, 1872–February 27, 1964): Founded the May Mortuary of Taylor, Williamson County, sometime before 1919. That year she was described in the Taylor section of the *Dallas Express* as "our popular undertaker," and she was recorded as an undertaker on the 1920 and 1930 censuses. In 1947, she organized a burial association in connection with her funeral home, taking on the role of vice-president. Her death certificate lists her occupation as a mortician.

MCCAMMON, LILLIAN FRANCES *JOHNSON* (February 8, 1882–December 3, 1962): Texas Historical Marker 7220 records that she and her husband, William Perry McCammon, renovated the landmark house Johnson-McCammon House in 1922 to make it suitable for use as their funeral home.

Texas Historical Commission Marker no. 7220 highlights the history of the Johnson-McCammon House. It reads, in part, "Originally built in the Second Empire architectural style, [the house] was altered to a classical revival appearance after 1922 by Johnson's daughter and son-in-law, Frances Lillian and William Perry McCammon, to accommodate a funeral home." *Mike Stroud/ Historical Marker Database.*

McCOLLUM, MATTIE WASHINGTON *GRAHAM* (September 30, 1872–November 20, 1952): In 1919, the firm of Hagey & McCollum in San Antonio was advertising a "lady assistant at all hours." By 1930, the now widowed Mattie was recorded as the proprietor of the funeral home on the census.

McCRACKEN, HATTIE FLO "HATTIE" *HOWARD* (July 21, 1879–March 12, 1961): After working for John E. Morrison Company for two decades, Mark P. McCracken incorporated the McCracken Funeral Home in Olney, Young County, in 1929 with Hattie as a full partner. The firm advertised her as a lady attendant.

McCULLOCH, CAROLINE M. *KEESEE* (February 3, 1875–August 17, 1956): The Zizik Undertaking Company announced in 1906 that it had hired Rush D. McCulloch, who would be "ably assisted by his wife in all calls for ladies and children." Subsequently, Caroline was advertised as an "expert lady assistant" and "the only lady assistant in San Antonio."

In 1906, Caroline McCulloch's employer not only advertised her services as a lady attendant but also offered a five-dollar prize for the best solution to the puzzle on the right. *From the Daily Express.*

McKINNEY, MILDRED R. (June 2, 1907–November 23, 1992): Recorded as the owner of a funeral home in Corsicana, Navarro County, in the 1930 census.

McMINN, MONTIE WINFRED *JOHNSON* (January 20, 1892–August 7, 1974): Montie married J.O. McMinn in 1912, and shortly after they opened their own funeral home in Childress. She was recorded as an undertaker on the 1930 census and a "helper" at the funeral home on the 1940 census. In 1933, Montie attended the conference of the Texas Federation of Business and Professional Women's Clubs. Despite her obituary reporting that Montie and her husband retired after forty years in 1952, after she was widowed in 1959, she apparently went back to work. A 1960 article in the *Grand Prairie*

Daily News announcing the new hires at the Dudley M. Hughes Funeral Home includes a photo of the small, white-haired woman working, with two young men looking over each of her shoulders. A year later, the Dallas City Directory listed Montie's occupation as an embalmer, and her 1974 death certificate listed her as a mortician.

MERRITT, MARY A. *COX* (October 28, 1906–July 16, 1957): Around the end of 1929 or beginning of 1930, licensed embalmer Mary and her husband, Charles L. Merritt, moved from Oklahoma to Wellington, Collingsworth County, just across the border, to work for the Goodson Funeral Home, owned by Charles's sister and brother-in-law, Viola and Ray Goodson. However, within a few months, the Merritts had taken a job with M.M. Nix & Company in Shamrock, Wheeler County, where the addition of a "licensed lady embalmer" merited a blurb in the local paper. The 1930 census records that Mary was an undertaker in Shamrock, but by the next year she and her husband had moved back to Oklahoma and opened their own funeral home.

MERSEREAU FRANCES L. "FANNIE" *BURKHART* (December 20, 1866–December 10, 1948): Recorded as an embalmer in Tyler, Smith County, on the 1910 and 1920 censuses.

MORAIDA CAPELO, ANGELA *QUIONES GUILLEN* (June 5, 1904–August 2, 1986): According to her obituary, she was in the funeral business for more than half a century and had "long been considered the first woman licensed as a funeral director in the Corpus Christi area,"[139] beginning in 1928.[140] Her first husband, the undertaker Tomas Moraida, died in 1933. Over the next two years, many obituaries in the *Corpus Christi Caller-Times* named Mrs. Angela G. Moraida in charge of funeral arrangements. In 1953, she and her second husband, Pedro B. Capelo Sr., founded Angelus Funeral Home in the same city. The business advertised her as the director until she was well into her seventies.

MORGAN, THENIA GERTRUDE *MATTHEWS* (September 10, 1868–March 14, 1954): Recorded working as an assistant at an undertaking parlor in Sulphur Springs, Hopkins County, on both the 1930 census and her death certificate twenty-four years later.

MOYER, HENRIETTA "ETTA MAE" *HARDWIG* (May 11, 1882–December 2, 1980): Entered the business in 1904 when she married undertaker Orville H. Moyer, who had embalmed President William McKinley after his assassination in 1901. She was advertised as a lady attendant with the couple's funeral home they started in 1909, later called the Moyer Mortuary. After her husband's death in 1948, Etta Mae continued in business and was recorded as a funeral director on the 1950 census. She sold the firm in 1953. Her death certificate listed her occupation as mortuary owner-operator.

NAGLEY MCLEAN, MINNIE G. *RAPER* (April 12, 1875–March 23, 1949): During a three-month visit to her parents in Illinois in 1899, Minnie attended two different colleges of embalming, receiving diplomas from each. The *El Paso Times* reported that she did this "in order to be of assistance to her husband in his calling." Speaking to a reporter from the same paper, her husband, J.E. Nagley, said that the firm of Nagley & Connors was

This El Paso undertaking establishment was built circa 1905–10. The "invalid car" on the right has the initials for McBean, Simmons & Carr, while the hearse on the left is marked with those of McBean, Simmons & Hartford, indicating that the picture was taken after the first business partnership folded and became the second in 1914. Both Mrs. Charles Henderson and Minnie Nagley worked for versions of this firm through the years. *Aultman Collection/El Paso Public Library.*

introducing something "entirely new to the city" with a lady undertaker. The business would advertise having the "only graduate lady embalmer in the Southwest" for several years.

PARKER, EMMA (January 20, 1879–November 1, 1959): When her husband, J.C. Parker, became a partner with J.P. Crouch & Company in McKinney, Collin County, the newspaper announcement was "signed" by Emma Parker as well and included the information that she would be assisting in the business. The company's ads often included a pair of portrait medallions of the couple. In May 1915, Emma was one of three women to pass the embalmers exam and earn her Texas license. The *Weekly Democrat-Gazette* reported that despite learning the trade from her husband and never attending a college of embalming, "her grade was remarkably good, having surpassed many men undertakers who came from other states and had been practicing the profession."[141] She was recorded as an embalmer in the 1920 census.

PEAK, GRACE EDITH (June 21, 1874–March 1, 1954): In business with her brother John W. Peak for forty years. Neither of the siblings married, so it was Grace who was advertised as the "lady assistant" and "woman assistant" at the various undertaking businesses of which her brother was a part in El Paso, starting around 1906. She was recorded as a co-partner in a mortuary business on the 1940 census. Two years later, the siblings retired and announced that they had sold their interest in the company to the third partner, Barry Hagedon, husband of lady undertaker Esther Hagedon.

PENN, EFFIE L. *MORRISON* (August 23, 1889–September 17, 1959): Recorded as the proprietor of an undertaking company and funeral home on the 1930 and 1940 censuses, respectively.

PERRY, ISABELLA *KELLUM* (May 14, 1887–December 27, 1937): Recorded as an undertaker at her "own business" in Houston on the 1930 census. Notably, her husband, William J. Perry, was recorded on the same census as a "helper" at the undertaking establishment.

PERRY, LOUISE GRAHAM *SCOTT* (September 22, 1866–June 24, 1953): Recorded as the vice-president of an undertaking company in Houston on the 1930 census.

Peterson, Mrs. W.B. (?–?): Listed as a bookkeeper and embalmer with the firm of Emerson & Berrien in the El Paso Directory for 1903.

Pinkston, Margaret J. "Maggie" *Lott* (May 1865–November 13, 1922): Recorded as an undertaker in Tyler, Smith County, on both the 1920 census and her death certificate. (The latter incorrectly marks her gender as "M.")

Price, Eva Jerome *Majors* (June 5, 1889–February 10, 1931): Advertised as a lady assistant with her husband Charles W. Price's undertaking establishment in Cameron, Milan County, in 1920. The 1930 census records her working as an embalmer at their firm, then located in Waco.

Quill Star, Jessie Lee *Wade* (June 2, 1903–March 24, 1959): According to her obituary, she attended the Dallas College of Embalming in 1918. Listed as a lady attendant (1927) and an embalmer (1933) with the Chas. F. Weiland Undertaking Company in the Dallas City Directory. (Charles Weiland was the husband of lady undertaker Cora Weiland.) Recorded as an embalmer on the 1930 and 1940 census, it was in the latter year that she co-founded her own business, the Marrs-Mundy-Quill Funeral Home in Dallas. She was listed as a funeral director on her death certificate.

Riddler (possibly Rudler), Heret M. (circa 1861–?): Recorded as a licensed embalmer with an undertaking company in McAllen, Hidalgo County, on the 1930 census.

Riebe, Mathilde *Hoch* (February 24, 1857–June 3, 1920): Recorded as the proprietor of an undertaking business on the 1910 census. Her then seventeen-year-old daughter, Ida L. *Riebe* Michael (December 24, 1892–March 5, 1971), was recorded as a stenographer for the funeral home in that census and as the company's bookkeeper in the 1915 San Antonio City Directory. By 1920, however, her younger sister Hattie Mildred *Riebe* Faircloth (August 5, 1895–June 6, 1958) had taken over the family business's administrative duties, according to the 1920 census. The census from that year also records that Mathilde had hired a young male embalmer, Mabry Faircloth, who lived with the family and would become Hattie's husband. The Fairclaths both worked for the Riebe Funeral Home for decades. After she was widowed, Hattie became the manager of the business, according to the 1950 census.

RITTENHOUSE, MATTIE PEARL *POND* (September 16, 1893–September 16, 1986): As the wife of Wilbur B. Rittenhouse, she is the most likely candidate for the "lady assistant, who is studying for the examination for an Embalmer's License," who was advertised in the *Palacios Beacon* (Matagorda County) in 1916. However, it is possible that this instead referred to his mother, Mary Ann *Fludder* Rittenhouse (October 16, 1859–January 2, 1938), as Wilbur's father, Daniel, was also associated with the business.

RIX HANKS, MARY WILLIE *DUVALL* (June 3, 1907–December 10, 1983): Married second-generation undertaker Ralph W. Rix and began working for the Rix-Griffith Mortuary. She was listed as the company's bookkeeper in the 1928 and 1933 Big Spring city directories.

ROBINSON PEEBLER, MAYME L. *BROWN* (November 10, 1881–October 7, 1975): Founded the Mrs. W.E. Robinson Furniture Company in Lubbock in 1907. In 1919, she announced that she was forming the Robinson-Simmons Undertaking Company with E.C. Simmons and that it would be opening at the beginning of 1920. But first, as the *Avalanche* reported, she was traveling to "northern markets" as far away as Chicago to purchase "the opening bill of goods" for the funeral home.

ROSS, ANNIE *MCCABE* (May 3, 1849–November 2, 1935): Lewis Ross and C.J. Wright were business partners in Houston at the turn of the century. After becoming a widow in 1896, Annie took over her husband's place in the Ross & Wright undertaking company, according to the 1900 census. Later in 1900, Annie and C.J. attempted to end their partnership but were unable to come to terms and spent several years in court.

ROSS, EMMA A. *BURNETT* (February 18, 1895–February 14, 1963): Recorded as the proprietor of an undertaking establishment in Calvert, Robertson County, on the 1930 census.

ROSS, SARAH JANE *HALL* (September 28, 1860–August 23, 1945): Advertised as a lady attendant with J.C. Ross & Company in the *El Paso Herald* in 1897.

RUDOLPH, EULA GRACE *STEVENS* (January 8, 1892–January 1989): The *Waxahachie Daily Light* (Ellis County) reported that she attended the Texas Funeral Directors Convention in 1929 and 1934.

RYAN, ALMA FRANCES *JATHO* (April 5, 1882–April 21, 1952): Daughter of the undertaker Adam Jatho of Victoria, Alma married Joseph Eugene Ryan in 1904 and brought him into the business. By 1912, Joseph was in charge of the company under his own name; in 1917, the company advertised Alma as a lady attendant. The *Daily Advocate* reported that the couple attended the joint 1921 Texas and National Funeral Directors Conventions in San Antonio.

SANDERS, LENA MYRTLE *GARRETT* (March 30, 1894–October 23, 1980): Was advertised as a lady attendant with the Rix Furniture and Undertaking Company in 1926 and with the Rix-Griffith Mortuary on the cover of the 1928 Big Spring City Directory (the same edition that listed Willie Rix as the company's bookkeeper). In 1929, Lena and her husband, Arthur C. Sanders, purchased an interest in the Rix business, which was renamed the Rix-Sanders Funeral Home. However, within two years, the Sanderses had struck out on their own, establishing a funeral home in Lubbock. Lena was recorded as an assistant funeral director on the 1930 census and a funeral director on the 1950 census and her 1980 death certificate. She was still working at the Sanders Funeral Home in 1970 when a newspaper ad called the seventy-six-year-old "A Definite Asset—Intuitively, it seems, Mrs. Lena Sanders knows just the right thing to say or do to make bereavement less difficult."[142]

SAUNDERS, ELLEN K. "MAMITA" *FISCHER* (October 21, 1905–December 27, 2009): By far the longest lived of the lady undertakers of the period, Mamita lived to 104. Around 1925, she began working for the Porter Loring Funeral Home in San Antonio, where she met her husband, Harold Saunders. The pair eventually bought the Riebe Funeral Home (which had been managed by Mathilde Riebe and her daughter Hattie Faircloth over the years), changing the name to the Riebe-Saunders Funeral Chapels. In a 1966 article announcing their move to a new location, it was noted that four of their fifteen licensed employees were women. Mamita was recorded as an undertaking assistant on the 1930 census, an attendant in 1940 and finally an embalmer in 1950, although she had first received her license in 1930. She retired in 1975.

SCHAETTER, HELENA JOHANNA *KOCH* (August 14, 1902–August 30, 1973): Helena married Arthur Schaetter in 1920, the same year he graduated from embalming school and joined his father Joe's undertaking firm. Helena also studied for her funeral director license, which made her the only licensed woman undertaker in Fredericksburg, according to the modern Schaetter Funeral Home. The 1950 census records that she was a mortician, and her death certificate lists her occupation as funeral director.

SCHWARTZ, OLIVIA *JACOBS* (August 29, 1868–July 4, 1950): Elected second vice-president at the Texas Funeral Directors and Embalmers Association in 1905. The *Houston Post* reported her in attendance at the annual convention in 1908. One of the fifteen Texas women undertakers profiled in the 1912 syndicated newspaper article. The next year, the *Laredo Weekly Times* mentioned her by name, saying that Mrs. H. Schwartz of the Schwartz Undertaking Company in Baird, Callahan County, had personally embalmed a Laredo resident, which was particularly notable since the deceased was a man.

SCHWENKE, MARGARET E. "MAGGIE" *SPRINGER* (February 1, 1877–February 20, 1943): After being unofficially associated with her husband in the undertaking business for more than a decade, she was made a full partner in the incorporation in the new version of their firm, Schwenke-Baumgarten Funeral Home, along with Otto B. Schwenke and Victor Baumgarten in Schulenburg, Fayette County, in 1933. (Victor was the nephew of Ottilie *Wolters* Baumgarten, who was associated with a previous iteration of the firm.)

SEALY, ADDIE W. (circa 1871–?): Recorded as an embalmer at an "embalming establishment" in the 1910 census for Victoria, Victoria County.

SHELLEY, VIOLA P. *SMITH* (November 19, 1871–November 12, 1923): Attended the Texas Undertakers Convention in 1910, where she was gifted "a beautiful shell ornament as the most popular lady" there.[143] When her husband, Joseph Shelley, died in 1922, she placed notices in both Spanish and English newspapers of San Antonio telling the public that she would be continuing their business herself. When she died the following year, her sister Lilly Ann Vodrie took over the Shelley Undertaking Company.

SIMMONS, MARGARET "TEDDY" *MACKENZIE* (1875–December 27, 1929): In 1906, the *El Paso Sunday Times* reported that Margaret and Frank Simmons had recently attended a school of embalming in Chicago, with Margaret subsequently passing the licensing exam in Dallas. They were associated with the McBean, Simmons & Carr establishment. In 1910, one of their professors from the Chicago school came to visit them in Texas. Margaret was of the fifteen Texas women undertakers profiled in the 1912 syndicated newspaper article.

SKINNER, MARY LOLA *WALTER* (January 27, 1889–September 15, 1962): Founded the Edinburgh Funeral Home (later called the Skinner Mortuary) in Edinburgh, Hidalgo County, in 1925 with her husband, Frank S. Skinner. She was recorded as a mortician on the 1930 census. She took on increasing responsibility at the funeral home in the late 1930s when her husband became unwell. In 1937, she attended the Texas Funeral Directors Association Convention alone. In 1939, she assumed management duties, and after she was widowed early the following year, she was recorded as the proprietor of the mortuary on the 1940 census.

SLOAN, ELLA FLORENCE *VOTAW* (1886–1968): The 1952 obituary of her husband, Samuel Dudley Sloan, noted that he founded the Sloan Undertaking Company in Fort Worth, Tarrant County, in 1911. The company advertised that it employed "a lady embalmer" in the *Fort Worth Record and Register* the following year.

SNEDDON, EMILY *BOYD* (circa 1852–January 4, 1917): Began working for the Wofford Furniture Company in Val Verde County, in 1906, running the new funeral department alongside her son Afton. Advertised as a lady assistant.

SPALDING, JENNIE LOU MOORES (March 27, 1890–December 6, 1976): Married Tom Spalding of Waxahachie, Ellis County, in 1909, and the couple subsequently worked for his father's Spalding Undertaking Company in that city. (Marie *Spalding* Niles [October 7, 1892–December 24, 1972], sister of Tom, also worked at the family business as a stenographer from 1914 to at least 1920.) In 1927, the couple moved to McCamey, Upton County, and managed the Harris-Luckett Company, a hardware store and undertaking business, before they finally opened their own firm, the Spalding Funeral Home, in 1936. They retired from the mortuary business in 1970.

SPANGLER, WILHELMINA MARY "WILLIE MAE" *TUMLINSON* (February 13, 1878–July 28, 1962): Recorded as an assistant undertaker in San Angelo, Tom Green County, on the 1920 census.

SPENCER, JEWELL (February 11, 1905–July 1989): Recorded as an embalmer at a funeral parlor in Terrell, Kaufman County, on the 1930 census and the operator of a funeral home in Sulphur Springs, Hopkins County, on the 1940 census.

STARKS, MAGGIE *FULLEYLOVE* (October 18, 1896–March 7, 1992): As a single mother, she opened Dodd and Starks (after 1931, the Starks Funeral Home), the first Black-run funeral home in San Angelo, Tom Green County, in 1927 with her husband's life insurance policy. The next year, she established the Delta Memorial Park Cemetery.

STEWART, ALICE (circa 1894–?): Recorded as an undertaker at a funeral home in Corsicana, Navarro County, on the 1930 census.

STICKLEY, MINNIE TALBERT *CAIN* (September 13, 1885–March 24, 1970): Founded the Stickley Funeral Home in Canadian, Hemphill County, with her husband in 1902, according to her obituary. The *Canadian Record* reported that the couple attended the embalmers convention in 1930, and the 1950 census records that she was still working as an undertaker's assistant after her husband had retired.

STONE EVERETT, MARY M. *HAWKINS* (September 23, 1857–June 25, 1941): *R.L. Polk & Co.'s Sherman City Directory, 1912–1913* listed Stone as the treasurer of the Fraternal Undertaking Company. She would later marry the president of the firm, Ned S. Everett.

SUTHERLAND, ISABEL A. "BELLE" BIRD (February 8, 1859–June 17, 1936): She was involved in the running of the Sutherland Undertaking Parlors in Corsicana, Navarro County, with her husband, Christopher Barrington "Bank" Sutherland, in the early 1900s, as well as being a hands-on member of the "ladies cemetery association," according to a 1916 article in the *Corsicana Daily Sun*, helping with the upkeep of Oakwood Cemetery. When she was widowed in 1928, Belle took out half-page ads in the same newspaper reassuring the public that the firm would continue under her control. While she sold it the following year, she stayed on as a director and the firm's vice-president and "serve[d in] an official capacity" until her death.

TALIAFERRO EALEY, NANCY NANNIE *THOMPSON* (June 8, 1882–June 23, 1939): Her husband, James Wood Taliaferro, was a licensed embalmer for the John

E. Morrison Company (the same firm that employed Hattie McCracken's husband). Nancy was advertised as a lady assistant with the company from 1909 to at least 1913.

TALLEY, GEORGIE W. (unknown): In its April 27, 1912 edition, the *Fort Worth Star-Telegram* reported that Miss "Georgis" Talley of Beaumont, Jefferson County, had passed her embalming exams. The article stated—incorrectly—that this made her only the second woman undertaker in Texas after Ella Fall of Waco.

TAPP, ZERVA *PATE* (May 14, 1881–October 13, 1974): Her 1989 obituary in the *Sulphur Springs News-Telegram* (Hopkins County) noted that she was the co-owner of the funeral home founded by her father in 1901. The Tapp Funeral Home advertised a lady attendant as early as 1929.

TAYLOR, CORAL V. (?–?): Listed as an embalmer in the 1915 and 1921 Dallas city directories.

TAYLOR SMITH, SAM M. "SAMMIE" (June 9, 1895–November 18, 1971): One of three women to pass the Texas embalmer exam in 1915, according to an article in the *Fort Worth Star-Telegram*. (The other two women were Susie Hewett and Emma Parker.) As a single woman, Sammie worked for her father's undertaking establishment in Temple, Bell County, where she was advertised as a lady embalmer after she received her license. She was listed as an embalmer in the 1915 and 1917 city directories, and she attended the Texas funeral directors convention in 1917. After her marriage circa 1919, Sammie spent a quarter century with the Guardian Funeral Home in Dallas, according to her obituary, as well as acting as director and secretary-treasurer of the Grove Hill Memorial Park. She was recorded as a mortician on the 1950 census, and her death certificate listed her occupation as a retired funeral director, having left the workforce in 1962.

THOMAS, JESSIE LEAH *BROWN* (December 8, 1893–March 19, 1986): Managed the Owens & Brumley Funeral Home in Burkburnett, Wichita County, alongside her husband starting in 1928, before opening their own establishment in Wichita Falls in 1937. Listed as an embalmer on the 1930 census.

THOMAS, LUCY ANEILIA *SMALL* (August 21, 1881–February 14, 1963): *A Collection of Memories: A History of Armstrong County, 1876–1965* claims that Lucy was "the first licensed woman embalmer in the Panhandle." Her husband, Charlie, and his brother Comer started a business together in 1902; after the latter's death in 1909, Lucy earned her embalmers license to take over the undertaking portion of the company, according to Charlie's 1941 obituary. A 1975 article in the *Canyon News* reported that she earned it in 1911, making her the fourth women in the state to have embalming and funeral director licenses. Lucy was one of the fifteen Texas women undertakers profiled in the 1912 syndicated newspaper article.

TUCKER, GEORGIA *ROYALL* (September 11, 1895–June 14, 1974): Recorded as a director of an undertaking parlor in Athens, Henderson County, on the 1930 census.

TUCKER, MARIE L. (November 21, 1890–October 15, 1974): Recorded as an undertaker on the 1930 census and a bookkeeper for an undertaker on the 1940 census, both in Fort Worth.

UNDERWOOD, MARGUERITE *PRINCE* (June 3, 1890–January 9, 1985): Recorded as an assistant embalmer on the 1920 census. During the 1920s and 1930s, she ran the Underwood Floral Company alongside the Underwood Funeral Home in Vernon, Wilbarger County. The combination made sense, and she advertised "funeral bouquets and wreaths a specialty."[144] She was record as a florist on the 1930 census, but by 1940 she was the assistant director of the funeral home and in 1950 the manager. She was also an owner of the Underwood Burial Association. After she was widowed in 1951, she placed a notice in the newspaper saying that there would be no changes and that she would be running the business. Two years later, she did sell the company, to one of her employees.

For about a decade, Marguerite Underwood was a florist and also worked with her husband in their undertaking business. As this 1921 ad shows, the two businesses were more complementary than they might appear. *From the Vernon Record.*

VODRIE, LILLY ANN *SMITH* (April 4, 1867–June 9, 1945): The sister of Viola Shelley. After the deaths of her brother-in-law and sister in 1922 and 1923, respectively, she took over the Shelley Undertaking Company in San Antonio. She was listed as the president of the business in the 1929 city directory and was also recorded as the president of an undertaking company on the U.S. census the following year.

WAGGONER, LORENA PEARL *THOMASON* (September 26, 1896–October 1, 1978): The Mont L. Waggoner firm in Stephenville, Erath County, advertised a lady assistant as early as 1924. Lorena was recorded as a helper at an undertaking parlor in Winnsboro, Wood County, on the 1940 census.

WATERS, FLORENCE F. *MCCARTY* (October 22, 1875–October 31, 1957): The *Victoria Advocate* reported that she attended the annual conference of the Texas Funeral Directors Association in 1929 and 1933. After her husband Louis Thomas Waters's death in 1942, she placed a notice in the same paper stating that she would personally be carrying on the business of the Goldman-Waters Undertaking Company of Victoria, Victoria County. This was the same company, under the name F.L. Goldman, that Leila Goldman kept running after the loss of her own husband in 1919.

WEADOCK, LENNORA *BIXLEY* (July 29, 1894–December 1971): Listed as an embalmer with the Houston Undertaking Company in the 1925 Houston City Directory.

WEILAND, CORA MAY *GOODMAN* (November 15, 1870–November 16, 1963): Her husband founded the Chas. F. Weiland Undertaking Company in Dallas in 1910. In the 1927 Dallas City Directory, she was listed as the company's vice-president, but after she was widowed later that year, she took over the running of the business. She advertised herself as a licensed lady embalmer and was recorded as president and proprietor on the 1940 and 1950 censuses, respectively. Her daughter, Alice Weiland Merritt, was listed as the secretary-treasurer in the 1947 Dallas City Directory. Cora was listed as funeral director on her death certificate.

WELLS, MARY ZUELLA "ELLA" *BARTON* (March 3, 1877–December 10, 1941): The E.N. Miller Company opened in Jacksboro, Jack County, in 1924 under the management of J.E. Wells, embalmer and funeral director. It advertised a lady assistant, likely his wife, Ella.

WESTHEIMER, LOVENIA "LOLA" *SPIERS* (March 7, 1871–July 25, 1954): Married established undertaker Sid Westheimer in 1902. In 1913, his eponymous undertaking company built a four-story building in downtown Houston to house its successful business. Lola attended the national funeral directors conference in Florida in 1917 and the Texas convention in 1918 and 1919.

WHEELER, LUCINDA ANN *JOHNSON* (July 29, 1867–January 17, 1944): One of the fifteen Texas women undertakers profiled in the 1912 syndicated newspaper article. The *Houston Post* reported that she was attending the Texas Undertakers Convention in 1916. Recorded as an embalmer in El Campo, Wharton County, on the 1920 and 1930 censuses.

WHISENANT, VALLIE *KOY* (December 28, 1897–March 8, 1986): The *Fort Worth Star-Telegram* reported that she attended the fortieth annual convention of the Texas Funeral Directors and Embalmers Association.

While Vallie Whisenant, *pictured far right,* looks rather dour in this photo from the 1926 undertakers' convention; the accompanying article said that the group was proof that undertakers were "a jolly group of fellows." *From the* Fort Worth Star-Telegram.

WILLIAMS, GUSSIE (circa 1907–?): Listed as an embalmer with the firm of I.C. Collins Jr. in the 1926 San Antonio City Directory.

WILLIAMS, JOSIE PAULITA *CAMPBELL* (October 7, 1908–June 8, 1975): After getting a master's degree from Prairie View A&M University, Josie earned her embalming license in 1927. She and her husband, Milton, founded the Peoples Funeral Home in 1923 in Marshall, Harrison County, eventually expanding to six locations, as well as starting the Peoples Funeral Service Insurance Company. Josie was an executive committee member at the 1931 Independent National Funeral Directors Association Convention. Her family believes that she may have been the first licensed Black woman embalmer in the county, possibly even in East Texas, although they have been unable to find conclusive proof of this. While Josie also taught courses at several schools and colleges in addition to her work with the family business, she was listed as mortician on her death certificate.

WILLIAMS, MINNIE M. (circa 1894–?): Recorded as an embalmer in San Antonio on the 1930 census.

WILLIAMS, MYRTLE MARY *VASQUEZ* (July 18, 1891–December 6, 1961): Recorded as a night clerk at an undertaking company in the 1930 census, a matron at a funeral home in the 1940 census and a night matron at a funeral home on her death certificate, all in San Antonio, Bexar County.

WILLIAMS, RUBY TEXAS *BAKER* (October 6, 1879–September 27, 1969): Recorded as an embalmer in Dallas on the 1930 census.

WILLISON, LILLIE ANN *JOHNSON* (July 1894–?): Recorded as the manager of an undertaking establishment in Waco on the 1930 census.

WIRT, MINNIE LENORA *SMITH* (December 25, 1878–May 12, 1946): Recorded as an assistant embalmer at an undertaking company in Houston on the 1920 census.

WOODARD, BERTHA *ALLEN* (December 8, 1895–February 29, 1984): Founder of the Bertha Allen Undertakers in Tyler, Smith County. In 1919, the *Dallas Express* reported that she had purchased a motorized hearse. The 1930 census recorded that she was the manager of an undertaking company.

WRIGHT, CHARLIE ETHEL *ROGERS* (December 1, 1884–May 1, 1970): Graduated from a school of embalming in 1911. That same year, she attended the Texas Funeral Directors Association convention with her husband, Tom S. Wright, and earned her license. She was one of the fifteen Texas women undertakers profiled in the 1912 syndicated newspaper article. Advertised by the Wright Undertaking Company of Temple as a "lady embalmer" and "lady attendant." Attended the national undertakers convention in Massachusetts in 1920. At the Texas convention in 1927, she was one of three women who received a box of candy from the Toothpick Club, along with Esther Hagedon and Annie Jennings. Recorded as a funeral home attendant on the 1940 census.

WYLIE, MARY ISABELLAH "MABLE" *JOHNSON* (August 20, 1879–April 27, 1957): In 1925, she and her husband, William Oscar Wylie Sr., purchased the Schwartz Undertaking Company in Baird, Callahan County, from Herbert and Olivia Schwartz. Recorded as an assistant undertaker on the 1930 census. Mable was involved in the business until she was widowed in 1942, at which time she sold it to her son and daughter-in-law.

ZACHRY, EVA EMILY *IRVIN* (July 18, 1884–September 23, 1951): Recorded as a lady assistant for an undertaker in Hunt County on the 1930 census.

ZENNI (POSSIBLY ZEUM), ROSE (circa 1898–?): Recorded as an undertaker at a funeral home in Plainview, Hale County, on the 1930 census.

NOTES

Introduction

1. Bess Woodruff, Scrapbook History of Mineral Wells and Palo Pinto County, book, date unknown, University of North Texas Libraries/Boyce Ditto Public Library.
2. Georganne Rundblad, "Exhuming Women's Premarket Duties in the Care of the Dead," *Gender and Society* 9, no. 2 (1995): 173–92, JSTOR, http://www.jstor.org/stable/189870.
3. Elizabeth Kytle, *Willie Mae* (Athens: University of Georgia Press, 1993).
4. "Undertaking Business," *Steuben Republican*, June 12, 1895.

Part I

5. "The Undertakers," *Dallas Daily Herald*, April 11, 1887.
6. "Funeral Directors," *Galveston Daily News*, March 16, 1893.
7. "Texas Funeral Directors," *Austin American-Statesman*, April 13, 1893.
8. "Funeral Directors Convention," *Austin American-Statesman*, April 14, 1893.
9. "Tips' Bill," *Galveston Daily News*, February 25, 1895.
10. "Texas Undertakers," *Houston Post*, April 2, 1899.
11. "Mrs. Sophie Jatho," *Victoria Advocate*, April 22, 1923.
12. Brittany Wollman, "Starks, Maggie Fulleylove," Handbook of Texas Online, https://www.tshaonline.org/handbook/entries/starks-maggie-fulleylove.

13. "Widow of Former Baird Mayor Dies in Cincinnati," *Abilene Reporter-News*, July 5, 1950.
14. "Yoakum's Lady Undertaker: Character of an Aunt Stars in Off-Broadway, 2-Act Play," *Corpus Christi Caller-Times*, June 13, 1980.
15. *Palo Pinto County Star*, July 31, 1903.
16. "Embalmers Return from Fort Worth Meeting," *El Paso Herald*, July 13, 1903.
17. *El Paso Herald*, July 20, 1903.
18. "Catholic News from El Paso," *Southern Messenger*, July 23, 1903.
19. "Deaths in Texas," *Fort Worth Star-Telegram*, February 16, 1963.
20. "McMinn Rites Will Be Held in Dallas," *Childress Index*, August 8, 1974.
21. *Cooper Review*, January 30, 1931.
22. *Cooper Review*, May 26, 1933.
23. "Announcement," *Delta Courier*, September 12, 1933.
24. "Dennis-Cumming Funeral Home Endorse Home Benefit," *Cooper Review*, March 30, 1934.
25. *El Paso Herald*, June 30, 1906.
26. "Modern Undertaking," *El Paso Times*, October 1, 1899.
27. *El Paso Herald*, December 6, 1901.
28. "Grief-Stricken Daughter, Who Left Mother, Blames Self for Parent's Death," *El Paso Evening Post*, September 8, 1930.
29. "M'Kinney Lady Now Embalmer," *Courier-Gazette*, May 21, 1915.
30. Schaetter Funeral Home, "Our History," https://www.schaetter.com/history.
31. "Blessing Funeral Home Marks 50 Years at Location," *Mansfield News-Mirror*, May 16, 1994.
32. "H.W. Kreidler," *Brownsville Herald*, September 1, 1941.
33. *El Paso Herald*, July 20, 1903.
34. "Catholic News from El Paso."
35. *Austin American-Statesman*, May 20, 1905.
36. "Woman Embalmer," *El Paso Herald*, June 20, 1899.
37. "Funeral Directors Honor Temple Man," *Fort Worth Star-Telegram*, October 21, 1927.
38. "City News," *Daily Express*, May 21, 1910.
39. "News 35 Years Ago," *Palo Pinto County Star*, June 30, 1939.
40. "Life Story of This Area's First Funeral Director…," *Hemphill County News*, August 5, 1952 (originally written in March 1950).
41. "Takes Live Ones to Get Dead Ones, Slogan of Undertakers, Who Spin Yarns and Jokes," *Fort Worth Star-Telegram*, June 7, 1922.

42. Texas Historical Foundation, "Death and Texas: A Personal Point of View," *Heritage* 3 (2016); University of North Texas Libraries, Portal to Texas History, https://texashistory.unt.edu.

43. "Timely," *Temple Daily Telegram*, October 31, 1919.

44. "City Brevities," *Houston Post*, January 31, 1899.

45. "Store Robbed at Grapevine," *Fort Worth Star-Telegram*, January 28, 1905.

46. "Sneak Thief Steals $40 from Funeral Home," *Vernon Weekly Record*, December 17, 1925.

47. The modern funeral home also suffered major fire damage in 2008.

48. "Fire Loss at Canadian," *Wichita Beacon*, June 17, 1910.

49. "Only Three Horses Perished in Flames," *Houston Post*, December 13, 1912.

50. Perhaps not surprisingly, after a stressful few months, Katie Lee Childs remarried, to Henry Newsome, in November and sold all her property before the couple moved to Nebraska.

51. "Fireman Stifled in Fire at Temple," *Daily Advocate*, September 12, 1917.

52. *Temple Daily Telegram*, April 6, 1918.

53. "Fireman Work to Pull Down Walls," *El Paso Times*, November 6, 1905.

54. The newspaper had some of these details wrong. The woman's name was Gussie Simon, and she died on the previous Tuesday.

55. "$100,000 Fire in El Paso," *El Paso Times*, November 5, 1905.

56. "14 Years Ago in El Paso," *El Paso Herald*, December 19, 1908.

57. Library of Congress, "Who Invented the Automobile?," https://www.loc.gov/everyday-mysteries/motor-vehicles-aeronautics-astronautics/item/who-invented-the-automobile.

58. H. Allen Anderson, "Carhart, John Wesley," Handbook of Texas Online, https://www.tshaonline.org/handbook/entries/carhart-john-wesley.

59. He also wrote one of the first sympathetic novels about lesbianism, which got him arrested for sending pornography through the mail.

60. "First Auto Builder Dies at San Antonio," *Austin American*, December 22, 1914.

61. "Prosaic Death Notices," *Wichita Falls Times*, May 24, 1934.

62. "Clyde Barrow to Be Buried Today, Bonnie Saturday," *Cushing Daily Citizen*, May 25, 1934.

63. "Boys While Hunting Make Ghastly Find," *Daily Herald*, December 16, 1912.

64. "Victims in Jail Fire Unidentified," *Houston Post*, December 1, 1924.

65. "Hundreds Stand Mute at Burial," *Houston Post*, December 8, 1924.

66. "'Who-Is-It?'—The Waxahachie Mummy No One Could Identify—Sent to Kansas City Museum," *Waxahachie Daily Light*, June 9, 1928.

67. "Human Flesh and Iron Are Sent Broadcast by Boiler Explosion," *Galveston Daily News*, March 19, 1912.
68. "Frost Death Toll Runs High," *Corsicana Semi-Weekly Light*, May 9, 1930.
69. "Frost to Bury Dead Today, Million Loss," *Fort Worth Record-Telegram*, May 8, 1930.
70. "From State Board of Health," *La Grange Journal*, December 26, 1918.
71. "Mrs. Julia Holman Dies," *Dallas Express*, February 15, 1919.
72. "Are We Retrograding?," *Houston Post*, July 20, 1899.
73. *Galveston Tribune*, April 2, 1904.
74. "Buried in a Shallow Grave," *Austin Statesman*, March 30, 1904.
75. "Paupers' Clothing," *El Paso Herald*, January 26, 1900.
76. "Given Decent Burial," *Lancaster Herald*, June 14, 1912.
77. "Undertaker in Borger Freed on Bond Today," *Amarillo Globe-Times*, October 18, 1927.
78. "Borger Undertaker to Contest Recent Charges," *Amarillo Globe-Times*, October 20, 1927.
79. "Undertaker Free," *Austin American*, January 11, 1928.
80. "Undertaker Is Sued in Death of Borger Girl," *Amarillo Globe-Times*, March 1, 1928.
81. *Fort Worth Star-Telegram*, January 3, 1926.
82. "Man Who Killed Girl's Slayer No-Billed," *Waxahachie Daily Light*, May 1, 1929.
83. "Former Mt. Pleasant Boy Charged with Murder at Texarkana," *Mount Pleasant Daily Times*, April 28, 1930.
84. *La Grange Journal*, March 14, 1901.
85. *Dallas Express*, July 12, 1919.
86. "Funeral Directors Hear Protest on Ambulance Speeding," *Fort Worth Star-Telegram*, May 19, 1926.
87. "Houston's Diversity Inspires New Takes on Funeral Services as Cemeteries Expand Rapidly," *Houston Chronicle*, October 24, 2022.
88. "Cremationists," *San Antonio Light*, June 13, 1885.
89. "Mrs. Emily Billings Dead," *Weekly Advocate*, February 10, 1912.

Part II

90. *Edmonton Journal*, August 28, 1912.
91. "Dead Cared for by Women Who Are Undertakers," *Springfield News-Leader*, June 23, 1912.

92. *The Province*, August 3, 1912.

93. *Wilmington Dispatch*, July 23, 1912.

94. "Home Sweet Home Is Sung at Payne Rites," *Brownsville Herald*, September 2, 1930.

95. "The Wages of Sin Is Death," *Cooper Review*, August 23, 1912.

96. "Women and Girls Viewed Corpse," *Houston Post*, October 29, 1912.

97. *Dallas Express*, May 3, 1919.

98. "Luz Calderon," *El Paso Herald*, May 22, 1906.

99. "Some Texas Towns," *Dallas Express*, March 12, 1921.

100. "Boy Drowned in Colorado," *Austin American-Statesman*, August 9, 1902.

101. "Lad Dies from Wound at Hand of a Playmate," *San Angelo Weekly Standard*, April 18, 1913.

102. "Tragic Accident," *Graham Leader*, April 4, 1918.

103. "Sonora Infant Dies Here," *San Angelo Evening Standard*, October 25, 1929.

104. "Why Women Shouldn't Vote," *Atlanta Constitution*, March 3, 1912.

105. "Life Story of This Area's First Funeral Director."

106. "C.B. Sutherland Died Early Friday Morning at Home," *Corsicana Daily Sun*, November 2, 1928.

Part III

107. "Undertakers Make Merry Near Coffins and Crepe; Black Loses Popularity," *Waco News-Tribune*, May 19, 1920.

108. "200 Here for First Session of Funeral Directors," *Fort Worth Star-Telegram*, June 6, 1922.

109. "Too Much Money Spent on Funerals," *Fort Worth Star-Telegram*, October 14, 1921.

110. "Funeral Directors Say High Cost of Dying Must Go On," *Fort Worth Star-Telegram*, October 14, 1921.

111. "Musical Numbers Heard by Radio," *Fort Worth Record-Telegram*, June 8, 1922.

112. "Undertakers Pick Waco for Meeting Place," *Austin American*, May 22, 1925.

113. "Horrors Gone, Undertaker Asserts," *Fort Worth Star-Telegram*, May 21, 1925.

114. "Funeral Directors Discuss Ethics," *Austin American*, May 20, 1925.

115. Ellis Arthur Davis and Edwin H. Grobe, *Encyclopedia of Texas*, vol. 1, *1922* (Dallas: University of North Texas Libraries), Portal to Texas History, https://texashistory.unt.edu.

116. "Undertakers Become Directors," *Fort Worth Star-Telegram*, May 19, 1926.

117. "Funerals Used to Be Cheap but Very Crude," *Fort Worth Record-Telegram*, June 12, 1922.

118. "Undertakers Become Directors."

119. "Egyptian Embalming Not Up to Present, Undertaker Asserts," *Fort Worth Star-Telegram*, May 17, 1926.

120. "Popular Beaumont Dog," *Austin American-Statesman*, May 7, 1911.

121. "Kills Monkey After It Terrorizes Neighbors," *McAllen Daily Press*, May 20, 1926.

122. "Accident Claim Paid," *El Paso Herald*, December 18, 1905. Willie Horner could not get away from death even when on vacation. While she was watching a performance at Carnegie Hall in New York City in 1906, barely three weeks into what was meant to be a months-long trip, her father dropped dead on the street outside.

123. *San Antonio Light*, April 20, 1908.

124. "Popular Lady Dies at Victoria Home; Had Been an Invalid," *Victoria Advocate*, August 27, 1925.

125. Jacob Roberts, "Coffins in a Bottle," Science History Institute, April, 18, 2019, https://www.sciencehistory.org/distillations/coffins-in-a-bottle.

126. "Society Notes," *Waco Morning News*, January 20, 1912.

Epilogue

127. "If 'Undertaker' Is Passe, Whyn't Say 'Mortician,'" *Waxahachie Daily Light*, May 21, 1930.

128. "Attends Convention," *Kerrville Mountain Sun*, May 22, 1930.

129. "Grammar School Day," *Victoria Advocate*, June 10, 1973.

130. "Malloy & Son Funeral Home Is Dedicated to Conscientious Service," *Galveston Daily News*, August 17, 1930.

131. "City Briefs," *Tyler Courier-Times*, May 25, 1930.

132. "Embalmers Elect, Pick San Antonio," *Fort Worth Record-Telegram*, May 23, 1930.

133. *Mineral Wells Index*, March 1, 1931.

Appendix

134. Jerry B. Lincecum, "Funerals and Folklore: A Snapshot from 1909," in *Celebrating 100 Years of the Texas Folklore Society, 1909–2009* (Denton, TX: University of North Texas Press, 2009).

135. *Houston Post*, June 29, 1924.

136. "Mrs. Griggs Funeral Set Wednesday," *Amarillo Globe-Times*, November 9, 1965.

137. "Daniel Heads Funeral Men; Meeting to Mineral Wells," *El Paso Herald*, May 20, 1927.

138. *Palo Pinto County Star*, July 31, 1903.

139. "Local Funeral Director Dies," *Corpus Christi Times*, August 4, 1986.

140. "City Women Have Made Significant Gains," *Mathis News*, October 22, 1987.

141. "M'Kinney Lady Now Embalmer," *Weekly Democrat-Gazette*, May 27, 1915.

142. *Lubbock Avalanche-Journal*, April 6, 1970.

143. "City News," *Daily Express*, May 21, 1910.

144. *Vernon Record*, May 13, 1921.

ABOUT THE AUTHOR

Kathy Benjamin is a writer, editor and humorist whose work has appeared on sites including MentalFloss.com, Cracked.com and Grunge.com. She is the author of *Funerals to Die For: The Craziest, Creepiest, and Most Bizarre Funeral Traditions and Practices Ever* (Adams Media, 2013); *It's Your Funeral!: Plan the Celebration of a Lifetime—Before It's Too Late* (Quirk, 2021); and *Texas Mass Graves: Burial Grounds of Atrocity, Massacre and Battle* (The History Press, 2022). She lives in Austin, Texas, with her husband, Simon, and dog, Briscoe.

Visit us at
www.historypress.com